A Fifties' Childhood

Tom East

Benybont Books

https://www.benybont.org/
First published 2020
Copyright © Tom East, 2020

ISBN 9781916297319

To Suki, Joseph, Edmund, Ping and Annabella

All names have been changed (or only forenames have been used with permission) but all the events and incidents are true.

ACKNOWLEDGEMENTS

I am grateful to JOYCE JAMES, plus members of the N05 and former 05 Groups (at various times JEAN BARRACLOUGH, JAN DAVIES, PAT FORSTER, ROWLAND HUGHES, CAROL JONES, DOMINIQUE SPEAREY and CHRIS WILLIAMS) for their comments and suggestions on the text.

CONTENTS

[1] Introduction – What is Memory?

The Oxford English Dictionary tells us that memory is 'the faculty by which the mind stores and remembers information'. Penelope Lively, in her interesting novel *Moon Tiger*, says 'We do not remember childhood – we imagine it.'

I don't think human memory is as mechanical as the dictionary makes it sound. Nor do I believe childhood is something of which we create pictures bearing little relation to reality. The other day I was talking to a group of friends on this subject. One of them said 'childhood memories are overlaid by later events' while another was keen to point out that there is much variation among individuals. A third reminded me that we tend to blot out unpleasant things that may have happened to us in the past. A similar thing to the first I've heard (I forget where) is that when you remember a past event, you are actually remembering the last time you remembered it, not the event itself.

It seems to me all of these things must have some element of truth to them. But the 'overlay' comment is really a less extreme version of what Penelope Lively was saying and I don't think the last has an especially great bearing on me personally: in putting this collection together I'm entirely positive I've unearthed memories that have lain dormant since their formation decades ago as well as those which have come to the forefront of my mind many times over those same decades.

We all know there is a huge difference between us in the extent and quality of what we remember. A group of people present at the same event will always take a range of recollections from it. Sometimes these can even conflict radically.

We should not forget the effect of inevitable subjectivity. Nor should we overlook the influence of what others may recount later on what we think we have experienced ourselves.

A personal example relevant to this point is given by the poem set out in appendix two. It concerns one of the earliest complete incidents of which I have memory. What happened was the father of my uncle (the husband of my mother's elder sister) fell on top of me. Much of the poem is most definitely composed from my own memory of the day and the impressions I had at the time; the physical description of the old man was exactly the way I saw him and the central incident took place precisely as I have it, right down to what my mother shouted and what I thought at the time (no, I didn't then have any real understanding of what 'I've killed him' meant).

But I should acknowledge that these memories were brought back to me in adult years by my sister's genealogical research years later on behalf of a cousin of ours. The event obviously couldn't have taken place later than the year the old man died, which was 1951 – for most of which I was aged three.

When I wrote it I was consciously writing a poem and was far more concerned with it from that point of view than with making an accurate record. For instance, I don't know that my uncle's mother was 'gin soaked', only (from other members of my family; I never knew her) that she was excessively fond of some form or other of tipple, to the family's detriment. She was herself from the Rhondda Valley; it was more probably this that prompted the family move from London than that her husband had 'heard the streets were paved with coal'.

And I didn't know exactly where the old man's grandfather was from. The 1851 census record said no more than 'Ireland'. He resettled in London during the eighteen-forties, so it would be a fair bet that the potato famine was the motive for the move: this terrible event in history I refer to obliquely by making his Irish home Tralee.

My sole justification for putting this collection of memories from the nineteen-fifties together is that I know I have an unusual memory with the power to recall incidents and other things in great detail from various times in my life.

In my mind are many images. Some are blurred but many are sharp and detailed. I have chosen to set down the earliest ones here because childhood is the time when our senses and impressions are at their most intense. This is the time that may give birth to a special kind of travel-writing, a time when our minds are at their most open to the wonders of the world. This is true even when those wonders could be found within fifty or fewer yards of our homes, no matter how 'ordinary' those homes may have been.

None of this is to claim I have a 'photographic memory'. If I am possessed of this mythical thing, mine has a cracked lens and a faulty shutter.

The 'classic memory' of people of my generation is the coronation of Queen Elizabeth the Second in the June 1953. I personally have absolutely no recollection from the time of the actual event. In all probability, many neighbours did indeed squeeze into our home in the oft-quoted style to watch the ceremony on our eight-inch television screen. If they did, the day didn't capture my imagination in any way.

We were one of the few households in our neighbourhood to have a television at that early date. In fact we'd possessed ours since the year before the Coronation. I retain distinct memories of a host of neighbours coming in to watch the University Boat Race in the spring of 1953. In those days, the Boat Race was an event attracting the interest of the majority of people, at least in London, who had never been near either university.

Although I have no memory of the Royal event, I vividly recall a 'coronation party' at my primary school a short time afterwards. I know the day was after the second of June, 1953: the party was on a fine day as opposed to the wet day of the actual coronation I've since learned about. At the school I had my first experience of jelly – these were the years of post-war austerity – and when I saw it trembling on the dish I thought, 'I'm not going to eat *THAT*.'

In 1990, I wrote a poem called *Memory*. I know many people don't care for poetry so I've relegated it to Appendix I. In the poem, I was trying to say something about memory in general by comparing early memories to building blocks. Those I retain are important to me, although I know many intelligent people who get by quite happily with far fewer blocks. Probably more important is the line, 'And in my hand is a paper packet'. This shows the association of ideas so important to the recall of every one of us.

Generally, the events happened as I've set them down in the poem. Yet, even at the time I put it together, I was conscious of 'editing the facts'. I was in fact seven years old, not nine. My view was that 'nine' read better. And I have many more memories of Clacton than the crisps and the big dippers but didn't want to water down what I was trying to say.

I clearly remember a toy yacht, my prize possession that summer: I broke the mast by hurdling over it, proudly but clearly not very elegantly. I recall going to a local fête as the guest of another family, the father of which won the 'knobbly knees contest'. My memory of the father and daughter is clear (aided by the fading photograph reproduced on the front cover in the case of the daughter) but I retain not the faintest recollection of the mother, apart from the fact she was there.

We stayed in a caravan painted in two-tone blue and cream called, unimaginatively, 'Bluebell'. It wasn't large but was luxurious compared with the tin can in which we'd holidayed in Porthcawl three years earlier. The Clacton caravan was situated on a caravan site called 'Highfield', though I'm sure I only know this because a few weeks later the young girl sent me a photograph with this name written in pencil on the reverse. The caravan park is still there, so the Internet tells me, though is certain to be grander than it was in 1955. Or perhaps 'grander' isn't the right word, now British seaside resorts have been so long in decline.

I really do remember the packet with 'East Anglia Crisps' on the side. It was a mention of Norfolk, which I knew (in 1990, not 1955!) is also in East Anglia that triggered the memory and gave rise to the poem. But this wasn't as casual a mention as I tried to make it sound. The discussion was in fact a detailed one with my wife. We were making plans as to where to take our two young sons on holiday in 1990. Every year, we used to have these conversations in the bleak post-Christmas period, so I can safely say I wrote the poem in January, 1990.

What about the 'overlaying' of which I spoke earlier? Although I have years-old images in my head, I know only too well that some of them may have been modified by experiences in later life. An important place for me between November, 1952 and July, 1959 was the hall of my primary school. To me, this seemed vast and spacious. Yet, when I had reason to revisit the hall not much more than seven years after leaving the school, I found it to be far from spacious. It was even cramped. The reason for my return was to take ballroom dancing lessons. It was something for which I discovered I have very little talent and so was keenly aware of the lack of space.

My childhood was undistinguished. I experienced no great events and nothing I could fairly claim as a trauma. Even the finding of a young girl's dead body, described in the last of these pieces [31], though certainly unpleasant, I could not in all honesty think of as traumatic. Perhaps this was because I wasn't told it should have been traumatic. The 'historic' events I describe, like seeing Bertrand Russell in Trafalgar Square [28] and hearing Sputnik I on the radio [24] were shared with numerous others. There are no dramatic or scandalous revelations to be found here.

No, my sole excuse for putting these pieces together is that they remain vivid and alive in my mind. I have tried to set them down in a readable way, though have made it a point of honour to record factually, purely according to my memory of what actually happened. I should, however, acknowledge that I telescoped three separate incidents in *The Yellow Omnibus* [26] I wrote this particular piece a number of years ago for another purpose and wouldn't want to try to unravel it now.

What I have felt at liberty to do more generally is to include a few reflections from a more mature perspective on some of the things I experienced as a child. It is, I hope, abundantly clear when I am doing this.

I make no claims for unusual precocity, only for a slightly unusual memory which I am now trying to share with you.

Besides events which have long been clear in my mind, I have dredged my memory for other recollections. I am conscious there may be some danger in doing this: I don't want to get stuck in the past. Nostalgia can all too easily trap the unwary.

A friend of mine believes that an infallible sign of ageing is when one spends more time thinking about the past than the present and the future. This may be true to a large extent, although I don't think it represents the whole truth. Socrates, who knew a thing or two, said 'the unexamined life is not worth living'. I am indeed grateful that my peculiar memory has given me a lot of life to examine, but have no wish to spend the rest of my time examining it.

What do I mean by 'the trap of nostalgia?' I believe it is too easy to see the past through rose-coloured glasses and want to live there. Here I think we would do well to keep in mind the words of the novelist LP Hartley, in the opening of his 1953 novel, *The Go Between*. He said 'The past is a foreign country: they do things differently there.' The key word here is *differently*. In the nineteen-fifties, the time when most of these events took place, things were certainly different. Not worse and not better, simply different. I've always tried not to look back at that different world through rose-coloured glasses, nor yet though darkly tinted shades.

The Facts

Since these pieces are concerned with my memories of the nineteen-fifties (with a slight overlap to the preceding and succeeding decades), I thought I should set down, simply and briefly, my main biographical details from the period.

I was born in late 1947 in Chiswick, London, the youngest of four children. My siblings were ten, twelve and fourteen years older than me so, in effect, I was the only child in a household of adults or near-adults of various ages. Shortly before I was born, my family moved to a new house in an undistinguished West London suburb. I was to live there for most of the first quarter-century of my life. Because I was still in the maternity ward with my mother when the rest of the family moved, this was the only house I lived in for not far off 25 years, although I know my family had many previous addresses, largely because of the disruption of war. Naturally, I have few memories of the nineteen-forties; save for one odd fragment that probably is from this period and which I recall in the first of these pieces.

Our home was in a small council estate, sandwiched between two areas of better-off private housing. Further to the west was a larger council estate, with a rougher reputation. The area where I grew up was therefore very socially mixed and I had friends from the whole area.

Council housing was not then regarded primarily as 'social housing' by either the public-at-large or the politicians in the post-war years. It was simply another place to live during a time of severe housing shortage. In later years many if not most of my former neighbours of my own generation moved away to private housing. Many of those of this younger element later took jobs placing them in a middle class that was to grow exponentially as the decades passed, or else they worked for themselves.

My upbringing was fairly strict, even by the standards of the time. In my case this was as well: I was one of those children who needed boundaries. But it wasn't in any way harsh and nor did my family have to face any special difficulties when I was young.

The house in which I lived was identical to the other twenty-six utilitarian houses in the road. Architecturally, there was nothing to set any of them apart from the other British Iron and Steel Federation constructions making up the estate and a great many like it elsewhere. Built in the year I was born, it was a new house. To me then, it was comfortable, though it was never centrally heated (this was rare in that era) and was distinctly chilly upstairs in winter. I don't remember ice being scraped from the inside of windows but I do remember hot water bottles.

Before I reached my teens we had no fitted carpets, refrigerator or telephone. We didn't even have a washing machine until the end of the decade. None of these things was particularly unusual. We were neither the wealthiest nor the poorest of the local families.

The state primary school I attended was a good one, with a more than usual share of dedicated and patient teachers. In me, they had a less-than-model pupil. It is probably best if I draw a veil over most of my full-time education, except where this is relevant to what I have recorded. Nevertheless, I should acknowledge my good fortune in this respect.

If I believe now the world was going forward at that time, I'm quite sure this is no mere nostalgia for my childhood. The nineteen-fifties was not only a decade of developing material wealth for most, but a time when more positive attitudes to the world were also increasing. If you think of it, things could hardly have been otherwise. The world was rebuilding after a deeply damaging war.

The scars of war were comparatively few where I lived in the West London suburbs, although I had to travel no more than a few miles to the east before they became numerous and highly visible. More noticeable to me personally were the constant verbal reminders of the conflict. In the nineteen-fifties, the refrain constantly on the lips of adults was 'before the war'. To me, this mythical time, like WWII itself, seemed

like ancient history. In fact it was in the recent past when I was
a child.

[2] Early Days

Ray Bradbury and Salvador Dalí have me beaten when they lay claim to memories of their own births. Apparently Dalí even said he could remember the time in his mother's womb. Still, I really do have a fragment of memory of being pushed along in a pram.

This may seem surprising, though perhaps it is not as surprising as may first appear. Prams have gone out of fashion now. Even when my sons were babies in the nineteen-eighties, prams were not often to be seen. Pushchairs were the preferred transportation for infants. Now these have developed into huge machines, more akin to sports cars than what I can think of as baby equipment.

In my own infancy, the years following WWII, babies practically lived in prams. They were wheeled around in them long after they could walk, so I couldn't say from when this snippet dates, although surely it couldn't have been any later than November, 1949, when I became two years old.

For me it can be no more than a tantalising glimpse of the decade of my birth. One of my brothers, ten years older than me, was pushing me along the road. Obviously resentful at his task, he pushed the pram and let it go. He didn't push it very far or fast, but it was enough to make me squawk in protest. And that is all I do remember.

Your suspicion might be that my brother was the one who told *me* about it. But, no, it was the other way around. To his great amusement, I complained to him about the episode when I was a toddler, only a few years after it took place. The pram in question, a black one, was kept under our staircase for some years after it had been used to convey me. It remained there until a neighbour bought this already aged piece of equipment, not long before I started school. Perhaps my later daily sightings of the pram reinforced the earliest memory I can claim.

The first memory *sequence* I still retain couldn't have been formed much later than the pram incident. My mother had to go into hospital for surgery. In those days, when the NHS was in its infancy, and for a long time afterwards, hospital stays were routinely far lengthier than those of today. My siblings were too young to look after me and my father had to go to work, so I was shipped out to an aunt, the wife of one of my father's older brothers.

Young children have few reference points and think any change is going to be a permanent one. My new abode didn't suit me at all. I couldn't stand my aunt's loud and high-pitched voice. She probably couldn't stand me either. With the benefit of hindsight, I have to acknowledge I was a difficult child.

Our greatest source of conflict concerned my potty. I was too young to use the adult toilet. I had a fear, which seemed reasonable to me at the time, of falling into its porcelain vastness, never to be seen again. When I first started to use the adult toilet, I insisted an adult kept a close eye on me throughout my performance. Not long before this, I was perfectly happy to confer my bowel evacuations on the potty unaccompanied. It was a steel or aluminium object no doubt of pre-war origin and used by my siblings ten or more years before.

Unfortunately, my aunt still possessed the wooden stool with a large hole at the centre of its seat (there was more hole than stool to the thing, as I remember) employed by her own son and daughter years before. The idea of this piece of baby-furniture was that the potty should be placed beneath it, so providing greater comfort to the children.

This in itself was no doubt a sensible plan, but I refused to sit upon it and showed my abhorrence of what I could only see as an instrument of torture with much stamping of feet and many tears. I was not capable of explaining to my bemused aunt that I actually preferred the cold reassurance given by direct contact with the metal.

After only a day or two, my father had to make the trek over to rescue my aunt and me from each other. My mother was still in hospital, so I had to be farmed out to another aunt, this time my mother's sister. Then, and for some years afterward, she worked full time and I have no idea how things were managed.

I have no more than a few shadowy memories of my time in her house, like the old-fashioned photograph frames of which she had a number. Part of their decoration consisted of a scroll-feature, which I fancied looked like a stick of rock and I wondered if I could eat it. Fortunately, I don't think I tried to do this.

The important thing was that my aunt must have been warned to let me use my potty in what I considered to be the traditional way, so there was no conflict between us on this score. Indeed, my mother later told me I was very 'clingy' during my stay with her sister. Apparently, I was unwilling even to let her go into the bathroom or lavatory without me, although I have no memory of such a thing. No doubt I had fears of being banished to my other aunt and her evil piece of wood.

My next memories, which couldn't have been much later this, also concern the infant NHS. This time I was the patient. I wasn't to be a very patient patient.

I had an ear infection, which our general practitioner gravely diagnosed as mastoiditis. At the time, this was a killer disease among children. Although it was already late in the evening, he advised my father to take me to a specialist hospital in Central London. Quite why an ambulance wasn't involved, I have no idea, but my father took me to the hospital by underground train. Because I was so small and young, he had to carry me for much of the journey.

The doctor saw me and was quickly able to reassure my father I wasn't a victim of mastoiditis. By this time, the hour was late, and the ward sister made the offer to my father to find me a bed for the night. This would avoid the need for him to make the long journey home with a fretful child. I didn't see things that way.

What I saw was an adult hospital that looked to me to be a dark, forbidding place. I wasn't having any of it: I didn't like what I considered to be the prospect of being abandoned and set up a noisy protest until my father agreed to take me home on the late night train. The last bus had gone when we arrived at our home station and he had to carry me for the last two miles. Even though I was only around two years old and not big for my age, I must have been quite some burden.

It seemed I did nevertheless have some kind of ear infection. Treatment necessitated a nurse calling in the morning and another in the evening to give me injections in the backside. This went on for a fortnight. Perhaps the first 'morning nurse' was gentler or a better practitioner than her evening colleague, but I quickly formed the idea that 'the morning nurse' was relatively harmless and the one who called in the evening was some kind of monster. Over the period of two weeks, there must have been some changes of shift and personnel but, to me, they were the same people calling.

In the mornings, I was entirely reasonable. But, if any knock came at our front door in the evening, I used to run up to the top of our staircase and anxiously peer downwards. If the caller wore a nurse's uniform I became frantic. Goodness knows how my parents persuaded me to come down for the injection but somehow we all got through the fortnight.

At the start of 1950, the aunt who'd rescued me from the wooden stool became a 'real' grandmother. The younger of her two daughters gave birth to the first of her sons. He wasn't really my aunt's eldest grandchild; there were two already living in America. They were the children of her elder daughter. These two, though, were largely known to her through photographs and letters, although she did make a few crossings of the Atlantic. The visit I particularly remember being impressed by was one of the later ones before aircraft effectively took over the crossing, made by *SS United States* in 1955.

The other reason this grandson must have been special to her was because he lived for nine or so years in the same house. There was a severe housing shortage in the post-war years. This gave her daughter and son-in-law no choice but to share the parents' home. My cousin was far older than me. I always regarded her as some sort of honorary aunt and her two sons (the younger was born a few years later) as my real cousins.

My aunt's home was only five or so miles from my own and we were frequent Saturday visitors to the house. On our first visit after my cousin had given birth, my mother naturally wanted to see the new mother and child. We called into the lounge, one of the rooms allocated to my cousin's family, only to find her breast-feeding. Whether my mother was expecting to see this, I don't know, but she wasn't flummoxed in any way. She turned to me:

'Do you know what they are?' she asked.

'Tits,' was my proud answer.

'You mustn't say that!' said my horrified mother.

I didn't know at two-and-a-bit and still don't know what answer was expected.

The final early memory I want to mention here is something I can date fairly precisely. In the early spring of 1951, I'd listened with my family to the radio commentary on the Oxford crew sinking in the University Boat Race. The next day I was shown photographs of this dramatic incident, in our daily newspaper.

A week or so later I was roused from my bed and told that 'someone special has come to see you'. Downstairs were two grand ladies wearing furs. Later, I learned they were Mrs Yvonne de Pfeffel and her friend, about whom the family only ever referred as 'Mrs Grob'. They lived in Brussels, where my father had been stationed for the greater part of his overseas war service. He'd formed a friendship with Yvonne's husband and had been to their house for meals a number of times.

I was told that they 'had come all the way from Belgium to see me, in a boat'. I marvelled at the thought of these two plump ladies rowing across the sea in a boat, no doubt wearing the same expensive fur coats. To me 'a boat' meant the kind of flimsy craft I'd heard of on the radio and seen in the newspaper the day after the Boat Race.

[3] The Call of the Sea: *[I] Rain and Snails*

It's a cliché that the sun always shines during the days of childhood. Well, it didn't always in mine.

The first seaside holiday I have memory of was in 1952. This was in Porthcawl. Despite the long decline of British holidays by the coast, this is still a popular destination for many in South Wales. My family were residents of London at the time so, as I recall our neighbours remarking, it was a more unusual choice for us.

This wasn't actually my first visit to Porthcawl. I'd been there in 1949 with my parents, sister and one of my brothers. That summer, we didn't actually stay in the resort, but in the nearby small town of Pyle with a woman who was a friend of my mother. When my grandmother was still alive, some years before I was born, she'd been her friend, too. I only ever knew her as 'Auntie Katie', although she wasn't really related to our family. She lives in my own mind still as an incredibly short elderly woman with button-bright dark eyes and extraordinarily rosy cheeks. The road she lived in has now acquired something of a 'Wild West' reputation.

When I visited again in 1952, as presumably would have been the case in 1949, it was perfectly respectable. I have not the slightest glimmer of memory of the 1949 visit; I only know of it because I'd seen an old photograph and quizzed my mother. In the photograph, I was a few months short of my second birthday, sitting fretfully on my unfortunate brother's lap. He'd not long passed his twelfth birthday.

I like half-seriously to claim I'd been to Porthcawl as early as two years before this. This might not be true in the stand-up-in-court sense because I was a foetus at the time. I only know about the holiday because my mother was given to repeating a few stories from that summer. My father had been discharged from WWII army service only in the previous autumn, so this would have been the first family summer holiday after the war. Quite possibly it was their first ever.

Two of the stories my mother told stick in my mind in particular. The first was when, sitting alone on Sker Beach (even today a quiet and undeveloped beach a few miles from the main resort), a man tried to 'chat her up', even though she was 'big in the way' (her words) with me.

Later on the same day, my family went to see the wreck of the *Samtampa*, a former wartime Liberty Ship wrecked on Sker Point in the previous April. The disaster had claimed 47 seamen's lives, despite an abortive rescue attempt by the Mumbles lifeboat, *Edward, Prince of Wales*. My father and siblings clambered all over the wreck. My mother, because she was carrying me, told me she could only climb a little way. Still, this was enough for me to make the perhaps dubious claim that I've been aboard the *Samtampa*.

The caravan we rented in 1952 was *tiny*. It seemed so even at the time to me, so must have been very small indeed. It stood with a number of others in a field of long grass, which was spectacularly wet. So wet was it that my parents bought a pair of Wellington boots for me. Equipped with these, I was quite happy to run around the caravan park whenever the intermittent rain permitted. Really, the 'caravan site' was nothing above a spare farmer's field, although I know it's been developed since.

I realised later that the farmer himself had a stunning resemblance to David Nixon, who was to become famous as the country's leading stage magician a few years' afterward. I seriously wondered if Nixon had worked the land before becoming a conjurer. At all events, he clearly didn't have the ability to make all that rain disappear in the summer of 1952.

Most of my time was spent playing in this wet field. One boy, with whom I became friendly, showed me a clockwork motor-boat he'd been given by his parents. Immediately, I had to have one. I wouldn't let my own parents rest until they'd purchased a similar model for me. Its clockwork motor purred beautifully and the single propeller whirred promisingly. But, when at last I was able to launch it in the sea, it sank ingloriously in the salt water. My father told me the clockwork mechanism was too heavy for the boat; by the time I got my prized possession home to London the motor was rusty. Quality control clearly had a considerable way to go then.

One day we visited 'Auntie Katie' in Pyle. I was fascinated by the fact that the main railway line to London ran at the bottom of her garden. It still does, although the garden is no longer hers; she died in the nineteen-sixties. I admired the speed at which the steam trains rushed past and fantasised about catching one to travel home: in reality I knew we were going to return via a coach journey taking eight hours and three stops to complete. The Severn Bridge was not to be opened for another fourteen years and the M4 motorway west of Cardiff not for another twenty.

'Auntie Katie' had a lodger who was a very keen gardener. He convinced me that, if left alone, the snails in his pride and joy would grow as big as horses. I was alarmed at this piece of information. They didn't do this in London; I was sure of this much. So I followed his advice and spent at least thirty minutes seeking out and crushing snails. I protested when my mother called me in for the day. There must have been more snails in hiding. Didn't they realise what would happen if the creatures were left unmolested?

We stayed overnight in the Pyle house. I was deposited in a big bed, amid awed promises I would be spending a special night in a real goose feather bed. What did this mean? I knew what geese were. They were birds that waddled awkwardly and made strange noises. Reputedly, they could also fly gracefully in the sky, although I'd never witnessed the truth of this for myself. With some trepidation I waited to see what would happen. Nothing did occur and I went to sleep.

The only unbroken sunshine I remember in the whole holiday was on the day we went to Barry Island. I thought I was in paradise with the busy fairground, the warm sand on my feet and the gentle lapping of the waves. Now Barry Island, like so many British resorts, is badly run down.

That first holiday by the sea has furnished me with many memories. The strongest, though, is of a day we spent twenty or so miles inland. My parents were from the Rhondda Fach, in their young day one of the foremost industrial centres in the UK. It was natural they'd want to spend a day there. We had numerous relatives in the valley but they chose to call at the house of a cousin of mine.

Our visit was unannounced; few people then had telephones. I believe our journey was unplanned, so there could be no prior warning via letter, the more usual medium at the time. The route from Porthcawl to the Rhondda Fach seemed incredibly complex and lengthy to me. Its last stage was a walk 'over the mountain', as my parents described it, though in fact I think all that happened was that we followed a hillside track at fairly low level. No doubt my mother and father were repeating an experience from their courting days more than two decades earlier.

We hadn't walked far on the track when the heavens opened. The heavy rain we'd seen so much of in South Wales chose this day to really show us what it could do. Presumably we had some sort of rainwear, but all I remember is being thoroughly soaked. By the time we reached the front door of my cousin's house torrents of water were dripping from us.

My cousin wasn't in. Fortunately, her husband was and he tried to refresh us with cups of tea while pressing us with drying towels. My cousin's son, still then a baby, played with his toys in the yellow-lit, gloomy front room. Most valley houses at that time hadn't been modernised; modern refurbishment has done wonders for their lighting since. My cousin's son ignored all my attempts to befriend him and join in with his games. I didn't mind too much: his toys seemed very uninteresting to me.

Oddly enough, I have no memories of Porthcawl front itself apart from my abortive attempt to float the clockwork boat. Besides memories of this, I have seen (and since lost) photographs of me with a bucket and spade on the beach, so evidently it didn't rain all the time. It seemed as if it did, though. It must have felt that way to my parents as well. After about ten days, they'd had enough and decided to cut the planned fortnight short.

My last memory of that holiday is of standing opposite the farm gate, waiting for a bus to arrive. Whilst waiting, I watched the antics of two exceedingly large pigs, just inside the farm gate. Then it started to rain steadily. The pigs didn't seem to mind.

[4] Early Day Women

Like most others, I was intrigued by activities of the 'you show me yours and I'll show you mine' variety. We called the more elaborate version of this 'playing doctors and nurses' or more descriptively 'being rude'. These games were played more in the spirit of scientific curiosity than prurience, although we knew the adults would have been horrified.

Still, I was keenly aware that girls were different, and I don't mean only in the physical sense. I must have been possessed of some early egalitarian spirit, because I didn't discriminate against females in the way most boys did. Although girls were always second-best for games of the 'rough and tumble' variety, and fisticuffs were severely frowned upon, I found girls could often be more interesting in the earnest discussions I also liked.

The first girl I got to know was called Sally Barker. She was at least seven or eight years older than me; at ten or so years of age this meant she was practically an adult. This was the key to our relationship. Like the other 'big girls' she liked to have an infant to drag and boss around. I must have been suitably compliant, at least to start with.

Sally, like many of the girls in her age-group, used to bore me with endless attempts at 'perfume making' in the garden. These involved, as far as I could make out, putting the petals of flowers like buttercups, daisies and dandelions into a small glass jar filled with water and then whisking vigorously. The more the water was whisked the browner it became. Sadly I have to report that *Parfum des pétales* never made it commercially.

More useful from my point of view, I was often dragged to places debarred to boys of my tender years. Two ventures on the same day Sally wouldn't look back upon fondly involved one of our local cinemas and a nearby park.

Sally and some other girls took me to see 'Saturday Morning Pictures' for the first time. The problem was, the illiberal manager refused to admit me. Children had to be seven before they were allowed to watch rescues from a railway line and similar adventures, or to sing the cinema's self-indulgent anthem, *The Greenford Granadiers*. I looked younger than my six years and the pleas of the girls failed to move him. It was to be another two years before I was allowed to join in with the chorus of *The Greenford Granadiers*. This still buzzes around my head today, even though the cinema made way for a supermarket in the early nineteen-seventies.

Undeterred, the girls took me from the cinema to the local park so we could all enjoy the pleasures of the playground. Apparently, my presence gave the older girls licence to go on rides intended for younger children. Unfortunately for all of us, they chose to place me on a roundabout and spun it quite fast. I was sitting in the centre, so was quite safe, but the faster it revolved, the more nauseous I became. Eventually, the inevitable happened ... whoops! Most of the girls screamed and scurried off, leaving poor Sally to trail me home in disgrace. I don't remember anyone clearing the roundabout of the former contents of my stomach.

My abiding image of Sally involves the 'pig bin' kept by the lamppost outside our house. These were the years of post-war austerity and, in the interests of economy and as an early example of recycling, there were a number of these food waste containers kept in the street along with the usual metal dustbins. I understood vaguely that their contents were collected separately and used to supplement the diets of farm animals. Sally's father was a baker, and my mother was horrified one day when Sally was sent out to dispose of a whole uncut loaf in the pig-bin.

The significance of this episode was that bread-rationing had been in force not too many years before this time (doing the arithmetic, I must have been very young). I was entirely sure I was going to be sent out to retrieve the loaf from the bin and bring it to our kitchen. The impression I formed was that the Barkers, wicked show-offs as they were with a baker at the head of the family, were wasting a valuable food that was still on ration. Bread actually came off ration in July 1948, well before I became an aware being.

My first 'girlfriend' of my own age had the name of Margaret, but was known universally as 'Blondie'. My mother and my twelve-years-older sister were very keen on her. Whenever they saw her playing with me in the street, they'd invite her into the house and make a fuss of her. Perhaps they saw her as the second daughter and younger sister they never had.

She had a brother, Derek. He was quite a few years older than us. His burning ambition was to achieve school leaving age. Every time I saw him he would spout off about getting a job to earn some money and, for some reason, 'growing a beard'. For years afterward I tried to rationalise this. Most of the adult males I saw didn't have beards. Was growing a beard some kind of rite of passage you had to go through before starting work? I didn't relish the prospect.

Blondie was a pretty girl who said little. She obeyed instructions in game-playing and was content to trail around the neighbourhood and passively stand by when I tried to show off. I am ashamed to admit this was too often.

Our friendship cooled after we started school. This was probably mainly because its time had passed, but the fact that we found ourselves in different classes was also a factor. After Blondie's disappearance from the scene, my mother and sister were always asking, 'Where's Blondie these days?' I couldn't answer. Nor was I really interested in trying to do so.

The practice throughout my primary school was to seat boys next to girls. Presumably the thought was that this would make the boys behave better, an idea only partially successful in my own case. My first partner was a girl called Hannah. Unusually, we could both read and write before we started school and were intrigued to see from the name cards we were given that each of us had two aitches in our names – hers in her forename and mine in my surname.

This distinction made us firm friends and I sought to please her by drawing a boat and developing a fantasy about building this boat in my back garden. I told her that when I'd finished, we could go sailing on it. Over the few weeks, the story spiralled out of control. Hannah was very taken with the idea and was continually asking questions like, 'When will it be finished?' and 'Can my mother/father/brother/dog come with us?' I tried to give reassuring answers, but was getting worried. Most significantly, I was concerned as to whether my back-garden would have been too small to accommodate the stupendous dimensions of the imagined boat.

Eventually, I had to admit that the whole thing was nothing more than invention on my part. Hannah was aghast. She'd believed every word of my story. Bucket-loads of tears followed and soon I found myself sitting next to a more severe girl, immune to my fantasies.

The policy of boy-next-to-girl was continued throughout my primary school years. A fair proportion of the girls in my class served their penance, though I only remember two in my final year. They were both called 'Pen'. The girls were not related in any way; nor, as far as I know, were they particular friends. One spelled her surname 'Penn' and the other 'Penne'.

Jackie Penn was a no-nonsense girl from the North of England. Susan Penne was an early martinet who was actually given official approval to slap me if my waywardness became too out-of-control.

The teacher made it plain that she had high hopes for first Jackie, and when she failed, Susan, to keep me in line. She was disappointed. I became firm friends with both girls. They became tolerant of my misdemeanours and I was always careful not to aim any at them.

Shortly before I started school, I had become friendly with another of the neighbour girls. This friendship developed. She was six, a full year older than me, and her name was Karen Williams. What I liked most about Karen is that she wasn't interested in playing silly perfume-and-flower-petal games. As far as I was concerned, she was one of the boys. She neither expected nor received special treatment.

Karen had a dog, an ill-tempered black mongrel called 'Charlie'. One day it bit me quite severely on the wrist. At this time I had an unreasoning fear of dogs, having also been chased by a mad Alsatian (literally – the poor animal was to die of a brain tumour) owned by one of our neighbours and a giant Poodle – it seemed pretty big to me - owned by another. Karen and Charlie played their part in desensitising my fear: later I became the owner of a dog, 'Mickey', a demented brown-and-white creature. The four of us became frequent companions playing dog-and-child games that would have been impenetrable to adult understanding.

The friendship of Karen and me survived the trauma of primary school. This was mainly, I expect, because of an unspoken rule not to acknowledge that we were on good terms whilst on school premises. But it didn't survive Karen's leaving for a senior girls' school. My own departure from primary school came in the summer of 1959 and, until puberty struck late in that year, my attitudes remained egalitarian.

In my later months in primary school, some of the boys and girls took to playing a game called 'kiss-chase', the object of which can be divined from its name. I wasn't among the game's enthusiasts.

It seemed entirely without interest to me. When, early one morning, one of the more developed girls approached me before the start of school hours, and demanded of me to 'prove I was a boy', I started to mumble about short trousers and so forth. This clearly wasn't what she had in mind, but I went to senior school as an innocent. Then, quite suddenly, adolescence hit me with a force like an express train soon after my twelfth birthday. But that is an altogether different kind of story.

[5] Post War

Right through the nineteen-fifties, the constant refrain on the lips of the adults around me was 'before the war', in the sense of 'we haven't seen those since before the war' or 'we had plenty of these before the war'. As far as I and others of my age were concerned, the war they spoke of might as well have taken place several centuries before. In fact, we were no more than a few years away from it. No wonder it still resonated all around us.

I had an entirely different perception from the rest of my family. My mother was full of stories about the war. For three of its five-and-half years, my father had been an enlisted soldier, seeing service in Belgium and Germany. He didn't in fact return home from Belgium until the July of 1946. His discharge and the very cold winter of 1946/47 must have led to my conception.

My sister and brothers were born a few years before the outbreak of hostilities. One of my mother's frequently-repeated stories was from the early days of the war, before she self-evacuated herself and young family from London to her mother's home in South Wales. On hearing an air-raid warning, the younger of my two brothers, then a toddler, would stand at the top of the stairs when the air-raid siren sounded, clutching a pillow and shouting, 'Kick Mammy, Kick! Hitler coming!'

Those years had gone before I was born. A weary world was rebuilding and the more time we were able to put between us and this ugly period of history, the better things became. Those in the area who had actually lived through the war might have seen things differently, especially if the conflict had touched themselves, their friends or families personally, but the part of West London where I lived was relatively unscathed by air raids inasmuch as there were few lasting physical scars. Most of the off-target bombs had been intended for the nearby RAF aerodrome, the only strategic target for the Luftwaffe in the locality.

On trips further east into London, mainly to see relatives, I couldn't help but notice the considerable effects of bomb damage. To me, though, these were no more than interesting sights, like the green buses that occasionally intruded into urban lands or the far more common glimpses of motorcycle-and-sidecar units.

My observations and my personal recollections lead me to believe the young accept almost anything as normal. Although there were plenty of other reminders of the recent conflict still around, I took them as part of the expected order of things. Rationing is something I particularly remember, because its impact finally eased only after I'd started school. I recall the constant moans of adults complaining about the fact that rationing and the accompanying austerity was going on for so long into peacetime.

Bread had come off rationing in 1948 but restrictions on the last foodstuffs (meat and bacon) were not removed until 1954. As a young child I took it for granted my mother had to take ration books as well as her purse when she went shopping 'around the corner' – 'going to town' or further afield to shop was a rarer event.

In exactly the same way, a weekly event was the visit of a large black van for the purpose of distributing free small bottles of what was considered to be strange-tasting orange juice to we children. This was one of the welfare initiatives of the time. It continued to be provided after the years of conflict to a population still suffering from the depredations of war, but I didn't then understand the finer points. All I knew was the orange juice was, to me and my friends, made from inferior stuff. Perhaps there wasn't enough commercially added sugar in 'welfare squash' for my taste and that of others of my age.

There were still many pill-boxes around and other concrete constructions left over from the war years. Underneath one of our local parks we knew was a large air-raid shelter and I was told, although I have no personal memory of it, the one from my primary school was only removed at about the time I started. We children were slightly in awe of these architectural remains, without really understanding anything of their significance.

Several times I went with my friend Jack and his parents on outings to the countryside. The main purpose of these was normally a shooting expedition with a twelve-bore shotgun. Legally, I suppose, this weapon must have belonged to his father but, in reality, it was my friend's prized possession. As well as being the de facto owner of a lethal gun, he also possessed an air rifle.

We happily used this lighter weapon for unauthorised random shooting on our unaccompanied expeditions or for target practice using paper targets. Often, because of their cost, we didn't have these and our targets instead became the large pennies of the time. If this sounds extravagant, it wasn't. The pennies saw battered duty in the shops after we'd finished with them. The outdoor shooting forays weren't something peculiar to my friend and me; it was quite normal for boys of nine or ten to own airguns and take them out for unsupervised use.

Even those of us who, like me, didn't possess an air gun of our own, often had an arsenal of toy pistols. The norm was a 'cap gun' which detonated rolls of 'caps'. These were small rolls of paper with gunpowder blobs which exploded with a retort and, if you were lucky, sparks or a flash. What I personally liked better were two plastic Luger pistols I owned. Lugers were the side-arms used by German officers in the recent war, something of which we were all aware but unconcerned about. What mattered to me was the fact that my toy replicas could fire small yellow plastic bullets at a good (and surely dangerous) velocity.

My pride and joy, however, was an authentic 19^c Navy Pistol, acquired from Goodness knows where. This could detonate half-a-dozen or more 'caps' at a time, with an almighty bang and a satisfying flash. I sold this after a few years for two pounds to Jack. To me, at the time, this was an enormous sum though the pistol would now be worth a thousand pounds or more on the antique market. It would also have to be deactivated. When I owned it, the gun could have been used for a more sinister purpose.

Looking back, it truly amazes me how easily toy and not-so-toy firearms were an accepted part of life in those days. When the world had only a few years before been through a terrible war, you'd think the adult population would have been anxious to remove all traces of weaponry. Plainly this was not the case.

WWI had come to an end only twenty-one years before WWII started and there was still a residue of the earlier war on the landscape. I am talking here about the human landscape. Numbers of old men, who had been damaged for life by the horrors they'd experienced in their younger days, still shuffled around the streets. I have a particularly guilty memory of two of these men.

The primary school I attended faced on to a main road, with the classrooms being separated from it by our large playing field, about twenty-five yards in width. Two WWI veterans often walked along the footway, separated from the field by chain link fencing about nine or ten feet in height. One of the men was short and tubby; the other was tall and thin. Both wore gabardine Macintoshes and peaked caps, the all the year round standard apparel for men of their generation.

Sometimes (I recall it happening three times) their passing would coincide with the blast of a teacher's whistle that signified the end of our 'playtime'. Immediately the shorter of the two men would fall to his knees. His friend couldn't persuade him to rise, despite pleas and exhortations.

We boys found this spectacle hilarious. I recall on one occasion a group of us being lectured by a teacher, who I think had seen navy service in WWII, about our disrespectful behaviour. We were told we should be thankful to men like these, who'd given so much in order that we should have comfortable lives.

I don't think any of us understood the moral significance of what we were being told. Certainly I didn't. Soon afterwards, the two men stopped passing the school. Perhaps they'd found another route to town. Perhaps one of them had died.

Strangely, we heard comparatively little about the recent front-line conflict from our fathers and the men of their generation. Most of them had seen the war in close-up. Only years later did I discover that my own father, but for a minor illness, would have been in a tank that was blown-up on patrol one night.

It was a sobering thought, to learn that I owe my existence to a cold or whatever this minor illness was.

[6] Comics

Not long before I started school in November, 1952, my glance fell upon a glossy comic in our local corner newsagent. I was fascinated by the grotesque green creature on the front cover and gave my mother no peace until she'd bought it for me. The creature was 'The Mekon', supposedly the malicious ruler of the planet Venus, and the comic was *The Eagle*.

When I got this treasure home, I was pleased to find it contained other delights, both in colour and black-and-white, like 'Luck of the Legion', 'PC 49', 'Riders of the Range' and 'Harris Tweed, Special Agent'. *The Eagle* was the brainchild of an enterprising churchman, Marcus Morris. Thanks largely to the panache he'd applied to the launch only two-and-a-half years before, the first issue sold nearly a million copies. This impressive figure was to increase substantially over the next decade or so. Such sales figures for a comic of any description would be undreamed of today.

As well as to the zeal of its Christian founder, the comic owed its success to lack of alternative entertainment open to boys. Television, then restricted to one channel, was in its infancy. I was myself deemed to be too young to be admitted to Saturday Morning Pictures. Major sports events were beyond our means and organised sport for children was haphazard.

Several months after I'd chanced upon *The Eagle*, my parents decided (no doubt after considerable prompting from me) that I should have a weekly comic of my own, delivered weekly. The one chosen was a 'funny' called *The Topper*, considered more suitable for my age group than 'The Mekon' and his friends.

Why I had this particular comic I don't know for sure, although it doubtless had something to do with the publicity surrounding the launch – I took *The Topper* from its first issue. I shouldn't think it was much, if anything, to do with the comic's large size. The pages were about A3 size rather than the more usual roughly A4. I have to say 'roughly' because the ISO standards weren't in use in the UK at that time.

'Mickey the Monkey' and 'Beryl the Peril' were decidedly less imaginative offerings than 'The Bash Street Kids', 'Lord Snooty and his Pals' and 'Rodger the Dodger', who lived in the pages of *The Dandy* and *The Beano*. These had been already long in publication in 1953. I realised this at the time but was quite content to remain faithful to *The Topper*. I even added its 'sister comic' *The Beezer*, to my weekly reading when it started up a few years later.

This might have been something to do with the paper banger pistol toy given away with the first issue of *The Beezer*, but the main reason I was content with what I saw as inferior products was that I could exchange them every weekend for copies of *The Beano* and *The Dandy* (50% cheaper) taken by the children next door. Once a year, a week or two before Christmas – they wouldn't let them out of their possession before this – they would lend me copies of the annuals they'd received the year before and I'd binge read. I saw this as part of the lead-up to Christmas.

Christian values of the time inspired *The Eagle*. 'Dan Dare, Pilot of the Future', The Mekon's wholesome nemesis, was originally going to be called Lex Christian. Someone must have decided that a good-egg British airline pilot, transported into the future and across millions of miles of space, was going to be a more viable hero. Unfiltered Christianity did make it to the pages of *The Eagle* in other ways, as in the colour strips features on the lives of St Paul and Jesus. There was a column called 'Mug of the Month' in which a reader was praised for deeds demonstrating high moral values. There were features on supposedly heroic characters like David Livingstone and the Conquistador Hernán Cortés.

As far as I know, the intended moral significance of this went over my head. I found my own heroes in the pages of *The Dandy* and *The Beano*. The latter in particular seemed to have genuine anarchic qualities. The fact that 'Rodger the Dodger' used regularly to consult a 'Book of Dodges' was a thing of wonder to me. He also had a 'weapons box' containing forbidden objects like a peashooter, a water pistol and a catapult. Naturally I too had to have a weapons box. As far as I know, my secret store was never uncovered.

A comic I also read most weeks a few years later was one bought for me by my sister on her way home from work on a Friday. This was the *TV Comic*, which in truth wasn't really very good. I liked it because it featured a character called 'Red Ray' a space roving 'goodie' whose inclination was to demolish aliens in various unpleasant ways. Nowadays we might say he was being very unkind to those who did not share his cultural values.

It was 'Red Ray' who induced me to make my only purchase through the pages of a comic. His magic coded writing set (I can't dignify it by its proper title because I can't remember it) proved to be nothing more than red and green coloured pencils and small cellophane squares of the same hues. The idea was to write your secret message in one colour and obliterate it with the other. It could then only be properly viewed through the correct square of cellophane. It was every bit as lame as it sounds. The only positive result was that it taught me to never again buy anything through the pages of a comic.

The generally harmless (forgetting the unpleasant things excused by old-fashioned Christian values) comics I have so far described weren't my first experience of the medium. This was with what was termed at the time 'a horror comic'. This gruesome thing belonged to the younger of my two brothers. He would himself have been around fourteen at the time. I know this was earlier than the spring of 1952, because I have a vivid memory of reading the black-and-white comic sitting in an armchair, sited where we put our tiny TV when we got it soon afterwards.

My father said to my mother, 'He shouldn't be reading that. He'll have nightmares.' They took it from me but they were too late. I did have nightmares. The featured story was of a man who stopped his car to give a lift to a mysterious robed figure (an inadvisable thing to do, surely?) When the two were driving along, the robed figure revealed itself to be a skeleton, causing the driver to go over a cliff.

Horror comics were a phenomenon of the time. They were shipped across the Atlantic in large numbers, both to provide ballast for ships and as reading material for the considerable number of American servicemen still here in the early nineteen-fifties. They found a much wider audience.

These comics led to outrage on both sides of the ocean. Marcus Morris was motivated to produce *The Eagle* in large part by his disgust at their content. Not so their artwork, however. Their influence on *The Eagle* was positive in this respect. In the USA the moral panic resulted, by 1954, in the self-censorship of the Comics Code Authority. In 1955 UK, legislation, in the form of the Children and Young Persons (Harmful Publications) Act, was seen as the solution.

My other pre-*Eagle* and *Topper* comics reading I remember with more affection. I found a taste for the small (roughly A5 size) black-and-white *Kit Carson* comics. These were nominally the property of the older of my two brothers. Kit (Christopher) Carson was a real-life frontiersman and scout up to the time of the American Civil War. His modern reputation is variable. Some portray him as sympathetic to the cause of American Indians, or Native Americans as they're now known; others say he was directly or indirectly responsible for many deaths among the tribesmen.

The comic unequivocally took the former view. I was particularly taken with the way his many Indian admirers (in the comic) called him 'The Yellow Hair'. Kit Carson would right wrongs with his plain speaking, a sock on the jaw or, if necessary, a blast from his flintlock. I believed every word.

I discovered many years later that, after his frontiersman days, he became a politician in the USA. Perhaps what I saw in the comics was the aftermath of an early example of political spin.

Horror comics were condemned on two main grounds and the accusations were levelled, with less vitriol, at other comic genres. They acquired a reputation for fomenting juvenile delinquency and of encouraging illiteracy. I am not qualified to comment on the former but the latter is definitely untrue in my own case. My mother had taught me to read a long time before I started school, but almost all of my early reading practice, undertaken independently and entirely willingly, was with *Kit Carson* comics and the like.

As the decade wore on I encountered numerous other titles. Among those I particularly liked was *The Phantom*. He lived in the 'deep woods' somewhere in Africa, and was believed by the 'baddies' he encountered and invariably got the better of to be three hundred years old. In fact, as only we privileged readers knew, the current Phantom was merely the latest in a line of Phantoms stretching back three centuries.

His favourite instrument of justice was an enthusiastic blow to the chin. This was no commonplace punch. It left a small, perfect, imprint of a skull on the wrongdoer's jaw. This came from the ring he wore. In the back pages of every issue I saw, there were advertisements inviting the reader to send for an authentic Phantom ring. I wondered about this at the time and still wonder about it. I even seriously considered sending for a Phantom ring of my own, although the disappointing experience of Red Ray's magic coded writing set made me cautious about taking this step.

An embryo social conscience on my part had nothing to do with my decision, I have to confess. The vision of trails of comatose small boys, each with a neat imprint of a skull on their chins, was distinctly appealing to me. Surely such an advertisement, if it appeared today, would fall foul of the Advertising Standards Authority, or even criminal legislation? If I hadn't encountered Red Ray some years before I might now know the answer.

In the later nineteen-fifties, I rediscovered American comics. They had shed their blood-curdling image and carried the 'Approved by the Comics Code Authority' logo in the top right-hand corner. Superheroes of either the *Superman-DC* or early *Marvel* (before Stan Lee) stables were the popular favourites with many, but I preferred the others. These were essentially toned-down horror comics.

The retail price in the USA was 10¢, which the retailers here translated to 9d (less than 4p). I tried not to trouble the shops too much. Most of my stocks came from a second-hand bookshop in Ealing, supplemented by a vigorous 'swaps' trade among we boys. Deals were prefaced by the enquiry 'any ten cents?' I was particularly active on this account and was a successful trader. If you said I put more industry into this than into any other commercial activity since, you'd be right.

Before the decade closed, 10¢ became 'still only 10¢' for a few months. Then it became 12¢ and finally 15¢. The shops allowed themselves generous rates of currency conversion. My interest in comics of all kinds was fizzling out by that time. This wasn't because I'm especially mean. Still less was it because my mind was opening to a higher class of literature. This was true right through my comics-reading phase.

I shall always be grateful for the part comics have played in giving me in an interest in the written word. My sight of that early issue of *The Eagle*, no matter what I now see as its moral doubtfulness, led to 4d (less than 2p) being well spent by my mother.

[7] Food

Today, I try to rationalise that food really was awful during the nineteen-fifties. I like to believe that if more care and imagination had gone into its preparation, I'd have been more open to culinary experiences, as I certainly am now. In moments of honesty, I don't believe, even if this were true, that it can wholly explain the bizarre relationship I had with meals during the decade.

The reek of over-boiled greens pervading the streets on a Sunday, the stacked steel canisters containing smelly school dinners (something in which I could never be persuaded to participate), the constant choruses of 'it's good for you' and the despair I caused my family with my perversity are things I now find wholly puzzling.

There were few foodstuffs I was really happy to eat. Some breakfast cereals went down well. I liked apples and oranges, though few other fruits. Certain brands of tomato soup took my fancy. Not all of them though; I was very choosy. The small triangles of many types of cheese spread were always something I'd try, though even here there was one brand I considered superior to the rest for no sound reason. There weren't many other things comprising my strictly limited intake. Even bread was something I tolerated rather than enjoyed until my mother brought back a wholemeal loaf from the 'Ideal Home' exhibition. From that day forward I would eat nothing else.

When I was younger, my mother and elder sister used to try to trick me by using manoeuvres like calling liver 'chocolate meat' or breaking a chip in half, then zooming it towards my mouth, pretending it was an ice-cream cornet. I wasn't stupid; I had a vague idea that chips were really produced by some sort of magic in the kitchen just as liver came from 'Jim the Butcher' (from where he obtained it, I neither knew nor cared). I can only reason that in some odd way I was conspiring with their imaginative device to get some nutrition inside me.

In the early post war years, there was a small range of soft drinks available for children. Most of the time, we were required to join the adults in their consumption of tea. This was sipped from a saucer when we were small. I preferred tap water, but this substance apparently didn't count for anything. Not until I was six did I discover such a thing as coffee existed on this Earth. Even when it came in bottles and had a high percentage of chicory blended with it, I found it vastly preferable to tea.

The rarity of soft drinks was no great hardship for me. The only things I actually liked were orange and lemon squash. Fizzy drinks I disliked and the various colas, very popular then as now, I actually detested. I still do.

Sweets have never been an important factor in my life, so it certainly wasn't the case that they distracted me from 'proper food'. In my childhood, I'd eat most of those that came my way as gifts. Chocolate Easter eggs always had appeal and I remember one Christmas being given a 'smokers set' (the mind boggles) consisting of liquorice pipes, sweet cigarettes and flakes of sugared brown stuff that was supposed to represent tobacco. I'm told now these were probably coloured flakes of coconut.

But, unlike most of my friends, who'd make a bee-line for the corner shop whenever they were in funds, I rarely visited a sweetshop on my own account. In the earlier part of the decade, I didn't have an independent budget. When later I did have some money I preferred to spend in on what I saw as more worthwhile things, like plastic soldiers, collector's stamps, model aeroplanes and public transport fares.

By the time I was eleven years old I was small and slight; I remember being told that at that age I weighed only four stones (56 pounds or about 25 kilos). On at least three occasions my worried mother, not at all a bad cook by the standards of the day, dragged me along to our family doctor. His response must have disappointed her. He told her not to worry; I was healthy enough and would eat when I needed and wanted to.

Both statements proved to be true. Apart from an early ear problem and mumps and measles, the last two at that time accepted as a normal part of growing up, I had few health concerns in my younger days. In fact, from my point of view, the worst things to befall me were mildly adverse reactions to vaccinations for Diphtheria and Poliomyelitis. At that time these scourges of public health were only just beginning to be brought to heel.

I certainly did start to eat much less faddishly once I'd entered my teens. During the early nineteen-sixties I learned to eat most things at home. From the middle of the decade I discovered most overseas countries had a more reverential attitude to the ingredients for meals. Forgive my unpatriotic comments but, talking about that time, I really do think the mocking caricature of Brits and food was deserved.

But here I'm talking about my strange behaviour in the nineteen-fifties, which can't be wholly explained, if indeed it can be at all, by this phenomenon. The worst time for me came once a week. I dreaded it.

I'm talking about 'Sunday Dinner', a ritual most families indulged in during the early post-war years. Many people still like the 'traditional cooked dinner' today. This occasionally includes me, though these days my vegetables are lightly-steamed or gently fried in oil to retain their taste instead of having their flavour and life boiled out of them.

For most of the week I managed to get away with my eccentrically limited diet. But it was the next thing to sacrilegious in our family to turn your nose up at the 'Sunday joint' and its accompaniment of mushy vegetables. The only parts of the meal I'd happily eat were the gravy, into which I liked to float a slice of bread, and the Yorkshire pudding. Time and again valiant efforts were made to get me to change my wicked ways. My only response was to make efforts to try to hide my meat under my potatoes and the hideous green vegetables. I found I wasn't able to overcome the basic laws of physics.

Every Sunday dinner ended the same way, with me being sent away from the table in disgrace after about ninety minutes. I breathed a sigh of relief when this happened, and enjoyed the brief respite. And it was a brief respite, too. A few hours later came the second food ritual of the week.

At five-thirty sharp we had Sunday tea.

[8] I Hate Skool

When I was three or four, or perhaps even younger, my mother used to look after a young boy named Paul. This was to enable his mother to go to work, something only a minority of mothers did at that time. She'd often bring us both small toys or other treats and I had a constant playfellow, so the arrangement suited me perfectly.

Paul was several months older than me, so started school several months before I did. I accepted this with equanimity; after he began his schooling he still came home at lunchtimes and was with me in the evenings until his mother returned from work. I was informed that before long it would be my turn to go to school.

This was a prospect I relished. For some reason I formed an image of school as a shiny red and green toy lorry on a shelf. This, for the amateur psychologists, was not in any way symbolic of home pleasures and comforts becoming inaccessible once I'd started school. The shelf of my imagination was low and the lorry was not a toy I possessed. If anything, the image was an anticipation of the joys awaiting me in school.

In early November, 1952, my mother took me to some sort of open or registration day held in the hall of what was to be my primary school. The purpose was for teachers, and presumably the headmaster, to answer any questions before the children started school, as major a step then as it is now. When it came to my mother's turn, she was keen to advise the man to whom she spoke (I know it was a man, but have had no idea who it would have been) that I wouldn't reach the age of five until later in the month.

'Oh, that doesn't matter,' he said. 'He can start on Monday.' I was happy with this arrangement. I would sample the delights of school a fortnight early.

The reality of school was to be different from my expectations. 'Toy Day' would have to wait until Friday. What was more you had to bring your own to school? Even then we were only permitted toys in the afternoon. On the Monday, Friday seemed impossibly remote. In the meantime there was the serious business of school to contend with.

The female teacher hoisted me up and sat me down close to a young girl, who was sitting in a circle with other children. She looked at me, clearly feeling as doubtful about the prospect as I did myself. I can still remember her name – Jane Islip – even though she was to be 'streamed' into the lower class a few weeks later.

'Do you want to sit next to this little girl?' asked 'Miss' (in fact I believe she was married, or about to be, and gave birth early in the following summer). My only response was tears, so I was whisked through the air again and plonked next to a young boy, with the same result. After two more rounds of whisking, plonking and tears, she gave up and left me where I was. This suited me as well as anything else would have done; I didn't want to sit next to *anyone*. I wanted to go home.

This wasn't permitted, although I did, in all innocence, abscond on my second day in school. The hand bell was rung to signal the beginning of the afternoon break. No other invitation was needed. I ran home as fast as I could. My mother was aghast. I'd come home over an hour early: even infant schools didn't finish until 4pm at that date.

My mother escorted me back to school (like most children then, I found my own way to school after the first day). The only response from the teacher was to laugh and to tell my mother she could take me home. I seriously thought of trying the trick again next day. In the event my nerve failed me.

After a week or two the desks were re-arranged into a more 'normal' classroom arrangement. My seat was next to that of a young girl, with whom I established a friendly relationship. Right through my primary years, the seating arrangement was always boy-girl, boy-girl. This seemed to work smoothly, at least at the infant level.

After a few weeks I settled down into the routine, even though I felt aggrieved about the lorry. Soon, I found my first school friend; my classroom companion somehow didn't count. Although I got on with her well enough, I associated her with the hated lessons.

Ian Blackmore was the name of my new friend. He'd started school a few weeks before me and he was *wicked*. His speciality was to show me how to collect spiders and cobwebs on a Y-shaped twig. Then, together, we'd chase the girls with them. The creatures were the small orange 'garden' spiders capable of delivering a tiny nip, so the girls had good reason to run.

Together, we got in all sorts of scrapes and the teachers must have thought we were headed for a lifetime of joint villainy. Fortunately for me, Ian left the school after only a few weeks more and I was able to make more sensible and longer-lasting friendships. Before Ian went off to wherever he was going, he did once come to our house. Rather, he came in company with his mother.

My parents had an ancient, leatherette-covered three-piece suite (obviously of pre-war vintage) they wanted to get rid of. As was the usual practice at the time, my father put a postcard advertisement in a local shop in the hope of selling it. The only respondent was Ian's mother, who came with her son to view it one evening. In the event, it turned out she couldn't afford anything like the asking price, which surely couldn't have been very high.

Before they left, Ian and I exchanged conspiratorial glances. Quite what we had to conspire about, I'm not sure.

Obviously this wasn't a view I formed at the time, but I now believe Ian's mother was a single parent. Women who 'should' have had a husband were frowned upon then. Why else would a woman come alone (this was the nineteen-fifties, remember) to negotiate a business deal that was clearly important to her? It might also partially explain Ian's waywardness. Something my father said, too, which at the time I didn't wholly understand and now can't quite remember has helped me form my probably doubtful adult view.

Who was his father? He may, like my own, have been a soldier returning from the war. But perhaps Ian's father didn't return, or if he did he couldn't settle down to peacetime civilian life. Was Ian was a different kind of 'bulge baby' from me?

alarming sermons of the severe-looking man who stood at the front.

I was instructed to refer to him as a 'Pastor' and not a 'Father'. 'Father Grey' shouldn't have been called by this name, anyway, so I was sternly informed. Worst of all were hints of a dark ritual lying ahead for me, involving my total immersion in water. I was seriously frightened by the prospect. Despite the strenuous efforts of my parents and the poor boy next door (my elder siblings studiously kept out of the debate) I couldn't be persuaded to attend this church more than a few times.

Now, in more mature years, I know myself to be agnostic. This is not at all the same thing as an atheist. An atheist is someone who is against religion. To my mind, this can be no more than a belief of a particular kind; an agnostic doesn't profess to know the unknowable. I have been agnostic for more than six decades.

Although I like to think my reasons for this are entirely rational, I have to admit that the foundations for my non-belief could have been put down in 1954 when they put up the first, flimsy, Church of St Thomas.

[10] Year Ending

Autumn is now my favourite season. It is a wonderful few months, not only for all the reasons inspiring so many nature poets over many centuries. Toward the end of it, knowledge of the dark days of coming winter lends an extra spice for me to the dying of the year.

When I was a child, the first part of autumn was nothing more than an annoying interlude between the school summer holidays and the truly important days of the year. These began at some time during late October. I'm not talking about Hallowe'en. This was passed over almost without notice where I lived in London; certainly there were none of the commercialised American imports we have today. No, I'm talking about the preparations for 'Guy Fawkes' or 'Bonfire Night'.

To mark the execution after torture of a rebel against the Government is a strange thing to do, if you think of it. Indeed, now in the twenty-first century, when we are used to seeing and hearing endless fireworks from October onwards, 5th November has lost most of its odd significance. You see more spectacular displays at the turn of the year. In the nineteen-fifties, those of my generation took the burning of the hapless Guido Fawkes very seriously. In fact, this Yorkshireman was due to be *hanged* on 31st January, 1606, but jumped from the scaffold and broke his neck.

Not for us the pair of old trousers stuffed with newspaper and hawked from door to door. You really did see this pitiful spectacle in the dying days of 'Penny-for-the-Guy' a few decades ago.

For most of we boys (only a few girls, so it seemed) the late autumn was the one season of the year when begging on the streets was semi-tolerated. When I was very young, I recall my mother's complaints about the number of boys on the streets asking for 'a penny for the guy'. I couldn't understand this. The question in my mind was always 'Why didn't she buy one for me, if they're so cheap?'

The other early memory I have retained of Guy Fawkes night is a physically painful one. Paul, the young boy I've mentioned in [8] and I were given a packet of sparklers to hold in front of the fire. I was disappointed when my first sparkler stopped and picked it up from the hearth to see what was wrong – by the red, glowing end. Paul was given the rest of the sparklers in the packet and the tradition of Bonfire Night was not celebrated the next year.

By the mid-fifties, when I began to embark on my own quests for pennies, I came to realise I'd misunderstood my mother's complaint. Still, we had to work for the money. One year, with the help of my brother's artistic skills and a few oddments like a pre-war grey suit and an old bus conductor's hat, I made up a guy to represent Adolf Hitler.

With my friend Jack, I hit on the idea that he should make a guy dressed up as a British soldier so we could take them on the streets together. I was very pleased when he was able to produce the goods. At the time, I thought the battledress he'd purloined or borrowed belonged to a WWI soldier. He told me years later he'd got it from his grandmother: it was her own WWII ARP (Air Raid Precautions) uniform. Never mind, it was khaki rather than the black you'd later see in the *Dad's Army* TV programme and it did come complete with a steel helmet that, with a little imagination, could have been worn by a soldier.

It looked impressive in its papier-mâché mask alongside the Hitler effigy and the two attracted the attention of many, both those who went along with our 'Penny for the Guy' motivation and those (mainly of our own generation) who didn't. I still remember two occasions when they received special notice.

One of the noticers was a boy of a year or two older than us. I knew him, although couldn't describe him as a friend.

In fact he was unstable and 'wild' and a few years after the day in question he was 'sent away' to some mysterious place. A small crowd of children were gathered around our display. They weren't paying but they were bestowing their admiration and praise. This was nearly as good.

The wild boy saw the attention we were getting, strode forward, reached into his pocket, not for money but his pen-knife, and then proceeded to repeatedly stab the Adolf Hitler effigy with it. Fortunately, a passing adult stopped his attack; otherwise there is no telling what might have happened. He may have ripped Hitler to shreds. Equally, if we'd protested, he could have turned his armed attention to us.

What did happen is that the adult, after sending the boy on his way, gave my friend and me a lecture, telling us how senseless we were to put such things on display so soon after the war. This was only a dozen or so years in the past but, to us, this made it ancient history. Still, we heeded his words after a fashion: we found another site where we thought a repeat encounter with the alarming boy less likely.

On another day later in the same week, we were astounded when a woman stopped and gave us a shilling for our efforts. This, five pence in today's currency, doesn't sound so much now but then it was a small fortune. At twelve penny bangers' worth, it was twelve times the asking rate.

Even more surprising to us than her generosity was the fact that our previous encounter with her was less than happy. My friend and I, together with half-a-dozen other children had a contretemps with her only a few weeks before. We were playing some sort of ball game in my friend's road: back then cars were no more than an occasional hazard in all except major thoroughfares, even those of outer London. The ball kept going over her front garden wall.

Twice she allowed us to reclaim the ball, but on the third occasion she lost patience, snatched up the ball, and strode into the house with it. This is not an unreasonable thing to do, an adult might think. But we were anything but reasonable. We were children of nine or so. Seemingly spontaneously, we set up a chorus of 'Witch! Witch!' It had no effect and after what seemed to me to be a long time we gave up and went our separate ways.

Although I felt uncomfortable about this even at the time (this is not me trying to put an adult gloss on our indefensible action) when I now think of what we did it makes me shudder. It was like a scene from a third-rate horror film. I often wonder if it played some part in making the woman give two of the young savages a whole shilling a few weeks later. Surely not?

After Guy Fawkes, the next 'special day' for me was my birthday, later in November. My experiences and observations lead me to believe many children think the World revolves around them. Certainly it was true of me, and this made my birthday a key date in the calendar. Naturally, many of them stand out in my memory. One is still particularly vivid after many years. This was when I reached the age of six. I awoke and was thrilled to find two boxes of toy soldiers on my bedroom window sill. These were what I wanted since I'd started school just over a year before and discovered from my classmates there were delights such as these in the world.

I was not more militaristic then than now, but the possibility of commanding platoons of my own was irresistible. Thinking about it all these years later, it seems to me that soldiers essentially served the same purpose for most small boys as dolls did for girls. The obvious differences may be more superficial than appears to be the case. Toy soldiers may provide an outlet for the aggressive instincts of boys, but both dolls and toy soldiers could be bossed around without fear of complaint. At all events, I was delighted to put my army through manoeuvres that would fill with horror anyone with Sandhurst training.

Until, that is, the heads of the models started coming off. First-aid with matchsticks proved to be unreliable and when bases also regularly began to part company with their figures, my military force began to look forlorn. The soldiers were made of lead. At this time, lead was still the material generally used. Plastic soldiers started to become more popular by the mid-fifties and lead soldiers were to be banned on health grounds ten or so years later.

I was happy to switch to the far more durable plastic as soon as I could and over the years acquired vast numbers of 'Cowboy and Indian' figures, complete with plastic wagons, tepees and the like. They were to become and remain my favourite toys, even though I was later to be given the three 'sets' that were supposed to be every boy's desire at the time: train, Meccano and chemistry.

It is a common complaint of men of my age that 'my mother threw all my lead soldiers out'. This didn't happen to me. My lead figures met their end at the bottom of a saucepan in late 1957. I was trying to melt them down to make lead spacemen, in homage to the orbit of Sputnik I. Needless to say, all I produced were shapeless blobs. I don't think the saucepan could have fared too well, either. A few years later, I gave my plastic figures to my young nephew. He proved I had overestimated their durability by the simple means of biting most of their heads off.

Important as they were to me, the days leading up to *the* highlight of the year paled into insignificance when Christmas actually arrived. It feels as if I can remember every moment of each of them from when I was a child.

The first Christmas morning I recall was when I was just turned three. I was startled into wakefulness, as were the adults in the room, by the noise made by my cousin Trevor, the next-youngest of our generation. He was six or seven months older than me and was staying with us, together with his parents and elder sister. Someone had made the mistake of giving him a realistic sounding toy Tommy-gun and a drum. This surely cannot be the case but, in my memory, it sounded as if he were playing with both at the same time.

This was my noisy introduction to Christmases in the fifties. After that, the magic of the festive season knew no bounds. The chief magician was, of course, Santa Claus. For most of the decade I steadfastly ignored all the young naysayers and was happy to set aside any doubts as to his existence, even if, in later years, he chose to leave my presents with those of other members of my family under the Christmas tree instead of delivering them personally to my bedroom.

At the age of ten I still wanted to retain my belief, even though the logical evidence against it was becoming overwhelming. On Christmas Eve, 1957, I slept alone in a small bedroom at the front of the house, instead of in the usual room I shared with my brother at the back (he was ten years older than me and no doubt celebrating Christmas Eve in the traditional young adult fashion).

As midnight approached I was having difficulty in sleeping. The competing emotions within me were taking their toll. Suddenly, I heard a metallic sound at the end of our short road. 'Sleigh Bells,' I thought. 'He does exist!'

Remembering all the cautionary tales, I lay still under the covers. But the sound grew louder, and I couldn't resist peeping through the curtain. There, beneath the bedroom window, was a group of 'Teddy Boys' kicking a tin can along the pavement.

[12] Door to Door

Callers at the door, unless we know or expect them, are anathema to many of us today. Witness the extraordinary number of warning signs in alarming capital letters underneath the bells or door-knockers.

Now, the only wanted people to knock on our front doors for commercial purposes are the milkman, now for only a minority of us and, if we're lucky enough to find one, the window cleaner. Thanks to the competition provided by the supermarkets, the few survivors of the once-extensive door-to-door dairy trade have huge rounds to cover. In the nineteen-fifties, we had a choice from several 'regulars', even in a short road like my own.

It wasn't only milkmen who were welcome at the door. My family and most of our neighbours would see the bakers' roundsman six days a week. Once a week our family had its main supply of groceries delivered by the owner of a local shop.

Prior to the Clean Air Act of 1956, coal lorries were a frequent sight. I used to love the sight and, more particularly, the smell of these. I'd make a point of walking past them inhaling the special perfume of the tarred sacks they carried. Empty sacks, for some reason, gave the greatest olfactory pleasure.

The coalmen rarely spoke but concentrated on their task of hefting hundredweight (one hundred and twelve pound or nearly fifty-one kilogram) sacks from lorry to house. Ten or fifteen years later I had a job which entailed lifting hundredweight sacks of rolled oats from palette to a blending machine and these were truly heavy. And I was required to manoeuvre them only a short distance. No wonder the coalmen preferred to save their breath

There were more irregular calls from the 'exotics'. The ice-cream van is still a frequent sight around many of our streets, but there were also visits from the likes of the muffin-man, the waffle-seller and the shellfish tradesman. Although they provided a service rather than a foodstuff, a team of men selling rides on tired donkeys and ponies around our suburban streets was a sight I recall.

Commercial travellers were treated with courtesy and often invited into the house. I particularly remember three or four lengthy visits by callers from the Indian sub-continent, who carried all their merchandise in a weighty suitcase (these were not fitted with wheels at that time). They must have relied more on their charm than the value of their goods. I remember their wares as being things like silk scarves, 'ties for Johnny' and worthless trinkets.

I particularly remember the visit by two men, who worked as a team for some reason. They were hawking around a solitary vacuum cleaner. I wonder now if it had 'fallen off the back of a lorry'. They were very happy to demonstrate the qualities of this machine. The trouble was, they had no plug for it. Nothing deterred, they inserted bare wires into the plug socket. The first electrical connection couldn't have been very stable, because I can still see the terrifying flash and loud bang they produced. Their second attempt must have been more successful because my parents bought the cleaner and were still using it (with a plug fitted) at least ten years later.

One category of unwelcome caller was the gypsies, carefully described by the adults as 'not proper gypsies, but tinkers'. There was a piece of waste ground near to where I lived. It was in almost continual occupation by successions of caravans – painted horse-drawn affairs at that date. Their owners regularly trailed around the streets of our area trying to sell wooden clothes pegs. 'Real' gypsies were widely believed to possess the power to put a curse on any householder who refused to buy their wares. I don't recall seeing anything that might qualify as this in action but I do recall one woman without clothes pegs who offered instead to tell my mother's fortune.

Most adults seemed to smoke in the nineteen-fifties. So I suppose it was only to be expected that some enterprising company should have hit on the wheeze of installing home cigarette dispensers. Our machine, which stood atop our meter cupboard under the stairs for eight or nine years, arrived when I was nine. It stocked two brands of cigarettes (no doubt at a generously marked-up price). 'Just in case' the helpful salesman gave my parents a key to its contents. Any unaccounted-for packets could be paid for on his fortnightly collection and restocking visits.

Can you imagine such a thing being tolerated now? The enterprise must have been hugely labour intensive, with its requirement to insert coins for change into the cellophane wrapping around each of the cigarette packets. Today, those at whom the service would be aimed would simply not want to bother with the fuss of it all. This is quite apart from any health issues.

It is probably no coincidence that my own earliest coughing experiment with smoking dates from this time. This consisted of a paper packet of four (yes, four) *Dominoes* purchased jointly by two classmates and me for furtive consumption in a field. I've never been able to find out what happened to the fourth *Domino*.

Apart from the boring 'rent man', other regular callers included the 'insurance men'. We had two of these. They called weekly to collect tiny premiums on life policies. It was the practice in those days to insure the lives of all members of working families. This, no doubt, was a harking back to memories of only a generation or two earlier, when child mortality was not a rare event.

Several years ago I found a 'fully paid up policy' on myself, issued by a large company whose advertisements are often now to be seen in print, on-line and elsewhere. These advertisements today offer maturity payments with figures ending in several noughts. The policy in my name from the nineteen-fifties was for the grand sum of twenty pounds.

Quite when the practice of door-to-door 'insurance men' (they were also called 'collectors' but never 'salesmen' I remember) faded out I'm not sure. I sold a telescope to one of our collectors when I was in my later teens, so it must have carried on until that time, if not for some years longer.

A decade or so earlier, I overheard a conversation between my parents and siblings which must have told of the demise of another practice from the past. At least, I thought it was in the past, until I discovered a few years ago it still survives in a small way.

It was something called by my family 'the clothing club'. The agent would issue a coupon for £10, £15 or whatever sum. Coupons could be used in shops, effectively as money. Repayments of a half-crown or five shillings (12½p or 25p) no doubt at a profitable rate of interest, would then be made and the cycle would start over again when the debt had been cleared or largely cleared. When I was very young this practice was widespread. You'd see the logo of the clothing club in most clothes shops. As the years progressed, however, shops probably grew irked at what must have been an arcane administrative system, and fewer of them accepted clothing coupons.

My elder siblings grew dissatisfied with the diminishing outlets available to them and agreed with my parents there would be no more 'clothing coupons' for our family. This would have been when I was about seven or eight. I am sure similar conversations would have been widespread in other households around this time.

Quarterly callers welcomed by all in our area were the meter readers. There were only two of them in those days, one each from the electricity and gas boards. Readers multiplied with privatisation and then drastically reduced as the new companies used agency contracts. Now they are reducing still further with remote meter reading.

Within less than a decade, things were to change, but until the mid-nineteen-fifties most households in my area had prepayment or 'shilling in the slot' meters. In times before my own, meters were fed with pennies in the slot.

Meter readers were popular callers because, as long as power hadn't been dubiously obtained with foreign coins or metal tokens, a handy cash rebate would be paid to the householder. The downside of this arrangement was that the house could be plunged into darkness if the meter hadn't been fed with its quota of shillings. This happened to us on times, even though we usually had shillings in the house because of my father's job as a bus conductor.

Neighbours knew this and made a practice of turning up on our doorstep with two sixpences, twelve pennies or whatever. On one occasion, the man next door came for a whole pound's worth (twenty shilling coins) from my mother. These he put into the gas meter. Then he put his head into the oven and breathed in the poisonous town gas.

We knew about the fate of the shillings – he obviously didn't want his exit to be ruined by running out of gas – because his widow told my mother afterwards that she had enough gas for cooking for a month.

Unusual callers, in the shape of police officers, came for a few weeks. The two elder children, the brothers, seemed to enjoy the celebrity status their father's suicide had conferred upon them. Their younger sister said nothing. She rarely spoke. Then, after another month or two, we found ourselves with new next-door-neighbours.

To me, the most interesting caller was someone we called 'the corn man'. He came at intervals of six weeks or so for a period of several years. This man was a chiropodist who came to treat my father's feet. As far as I know, my father didn't have a particular foot problem. I can only assume chiropody was one of the few luxuries he indulged in.

The array of steel instruments was fascinating to me. I'd watch the corn man at work as if he were some sort of magician. When I learned that another of his customers was 'the BBC' I was absolutely sure he was a magician. I assumed he'd know everything there was to know about television programmes and used to bombard him with questions.

One topic that particularly bothered me was how so many people could be shot in TV westerns: I really thought that people were actually killed for our entertainment (I should say in my defence we'd had a television since I was four-and-a-bit; so I should think I was young at the time). Naturally, I put my concerns to our friendly corn man.

He must have been perplexed by my question, because he told me that the BBC chose people who were ill and knew they didn't have long to live. This puzzled me. There seemed to be a lot of sick people about. Should they be doing things like riding horses at a gallop, if they were unwell? Despite all the contradictions I could see, I believed him implicitly. He was our corn man and worked at the BBC. I shared my inside knowledge with several friends. It was at least a year before I could be persuaded to accept a more rational explanation.

[13] Family Matters

My parents were born in neighbouring villages in the Rhondda Fach, South Wales. At the time of their births, this was one of the boom industrial areas in the United Kingdom. Like most people who say they have their roots 'in the Rhondda', their real antecedents go back to other places. Both Rhondda Valleys began their dynamic growth only in the mid nineteenth century, when coal pits began to be sunk on a vast scale.

Three of my grandparents moved, as children with their families, to the Rhonda Fach about thirty years after its first growth. My paternal grandfather was the exception. He went to the valley on his own, as a very young man seeking work.

My 'name' ancestors had actually spent several generations in another industrial area, the Black Country of the English West Midlands. However, since the marriage of my paternal grandfather's parents lasted no more than a few years, after which my great-grandmother fled homewards to Mid Wales with her only son, I feel no particular connection with the West Midlands.

My grandfather was raised in Newtown, Montgomeryshire as a first-language Welsh speaker. He was a teenager when he went to the Rhondda Fach for work and was still in his teens when he married my maternal grandmother. She was born in Swansea when her family were being drawn eastward from a more rural setting in Carmarthenshire. They'd lived there for generations, working as masons.

There were no such complications with my mother's family. Both sides of this had lived rural existences in Mid Wales before they too were sucked into the industrialisation further south.

My sister Mary studied all this in great depth over nearly forty years so I now know a great deal of detail about my family background. However, even as a child living in London (to where the family had moved to seek better fortune in 1936, well before I was born) I knew the general outlines of the story.

I was aware of it from things my mother told me and from her accumulation of old photographs, mainly sepia-tinted. As far as I was concerned 'family' meant my parents, siblings and me, plus those of my uncles and aunts who'd themselves made the move to London for work. This was about a third of a large number. Most of their children, my cousins, were born in Wales, but had resettled in London when they were young. Almost all of my cousins were considerably older than me and I looked upon them as more a species of honorary uncle or aunt than as the members of my own generation they in fact were.

My brothers and sister were also older than me by ten or more years so I regarded them, as indeed they were, young adults who shared the house with me. Being born prior to the outbreak of WWII (I was a post-war baby-boomer) also meant their childhoods were severely disrupted by the outbreak of war only a few years after the family moved to London, with a private evacuation to relatives in the Rhondda Fach and finally a move back to London when hostilities were over but the country was left with a considerable housing shortage. Not until shortly before I arrived on the scene in 1947 did the family find more permanent accommodation. I was the lucky one.

So, in many ways my life was like that of an only child, aware of his Welsh background, even though it meant little more to that child than the photographs kept in a cardboard box.

*

It was therefore more of a surprise than anything else when my maternal grandfather emerged from this sepia tint. The picture of him as a young soldier in WWI uniform is one of the photographs that especially caught my young imagination. He, David Rees Thomas, came to stay at our home for a fortnight in the summer of 1959.

He'd been the only one of my grandparents who was still alive at the time of my birth. In fact he'd become estranged from my mother and her siblings following his remarriage soon after my grandmother's death, We'd had no contact with him until he and my mother exchanged a few letters earlier that year.

With him he brought his adopted son, Terry. The young, very blond, boy was only a few years older than me and I liked to infuriate him by introducing him to my friends as 'my Uncle Terry'. My grandfather used to take Terry and me for long walks.

He was fascinated by the differences between his native Rhondda Fach and London. After all, the only time he'd been out of South Wales previously was in WWI. In all respects he was an interested and interesting man and I enjoyed the two weeks when I had a grandparent like my friends.

For no particular reason, the thing that sticks in my mind is that he wanted to know who 'Lady Margaret Road', a nearby minor shopping street, had been named after. To my shame I couldn't supply the answer to his question. Later, through my persistent interrogation of the adults around me, I discovered this was Lady Margaret Beaufort, a grandmother of King Henry VIII. She'd been very influential in the Wars of the Roses and William Caxton's early efforts in printing. I wonder how many of today's residents of Lady Margaret Road know anything about the origin of its name?

Although my grandfather had been hale and hearty in the summer of 1959, he was to die only eighteen months later. I saw him on just this one occasion before he slipped back into the box of sepia photographs. Then, to me, 'family' was restored to the narrow definition I'd been used to for over eleven years.

[14] Frightening the Children

The British Board of Film Classification (until 1985, the 'C' stood for 'Censors') was founded as long ago as 1912, so I am at a loss as to how I came to be watching a 3D horror film at the age of four or five.

Perhaps the BBFC had a different emphasis in the post-war years. Perhaps what I saw wasn't regarded as a true horror film. It may have been a comedy or even a short demonstrating the capabilities of 3D film, very popular at the time. The early nineteen-fifties were something of a golden age for three dimensional cinema, even though the technology would be regarded as crude now. The cardboard and cellophane red-green spectacles through which the film had to be viewed were flimsy and most definitely designed for single use.

At all events, what I saw was utterly realistic as far as I was concerned. I screamed mightily as the skeleton atop a burning roof hurled down fiery slates towards the cinema audience. I was persuaded to duck down behind the seat until the crisis had passed. But, when what was presumably the main feature came on, I started to scream again. This was because the innocent black-and-white film we saw had an opening scene vaguely similar to that of the yellow skeleton's film. I was convinced that the young woman knocking at the door of the large house would before long encounter another hideous being.

This little drama took place in what was by far the swisher of the two cinemas in our town. The other was a frankly flea-bitten place. It had been built not much more than thirty years before, but no visitor to *The Playhouse* would have believed this. On one occasion, a year or two after the skeleton had given me unlooked-for entertainment and I'd given unwanted entertainment to the cinema audience, I'd gone to *The Playhouse* to see two perfectly harmless cartoons with my parents. During the intermission – there normally was one between the two features then – I'd decided to visit the loo, a dimly lit place tucked away in labyrinthine corridors near to the front.

As I approached the outer door, a youth emerged. Possibly the effect was enhanced by the lighting – the half-light of the auditorium in combination with the pale yellow backlight from the gents – but his appearance startled me in an extraordinary way. He had sparse blond hair, sallow skin and enormous dark rings around his eyes. His expression was, or seemed to me to be, one of abject misery. Most probably the poor boy was or had been ill, but I was convinced I'd seen a ghost. I turned back, to the bemusement of my parents, and didn't ease my bladder until I reached home some time later.

We children must have enjoyed being frightened. My favourite rhyme (I only ever heard it, never saw it in print) was this one:

> *Mrs White*
> *had a fright*
> *in the middle of the night.*
> *Saw a ghost*
> *eating toast*
> *half way up the lamppost.*

Clearly this was intended to be humorous, but I didn't see it that way. Every time I heard or thought of the rhyme the words created in my mind an image of a spectral figure, a kind of blurred skeleton, clinging to a lamppost. The thing wasn't laughing. It was grinning alarmingly, as if to say 'I'll be down for you in a minute'. Whenever I looked out of our landing window in the night I more than half-expected to see this figure leering back at me from his perch. The streets then were lit by none-too-luminous white street lamps; the modern, friendlier amber lights weren't to arrive for another few years and the old street lighting shone with a far dimmer light than the white lamps we now have. The pale illumination would have set my imagined ghost off perfectly.

I was by no means alone in having a dark side to my imagination. In the earlier nineteen-fifties there were only a handful of brands of breakfast cereal available. These didn't begin their exponential multiplication until later in the decade, when greater prosperity started to arrive. Rarer still were the soon-to-be-common giveaway extras like plastic toys at the bottom of the packets.

This marketing ploy, when it arrived, worked like a charm on me. In fact it was successful starting with what must have been its prototype, the low cost wheeze of printing a mask on the back of the cereal packet. Although I didn't like the taste of the particular cereal, I persuaded my mother to buy several packets and munched my way through their contents simply to get my hands on the cut-out masks. My ambition was to be eligible to join the group of local children who wore masks in the street with the usually successful aim of scaring each other with them.

The prized possession was a grotesque Devil's mask. Donning this was a passport to macabre delight. As far as we were concerned, the wearer *became* the Devil and was granted free licence to make everyone scream. This mask was followed in popularity by that of an indeterminate being, somewhere between an Egyptian mummy, a corpse and a Frankenstein's monster. No-one really knew what this was supposed to be, but it clearly belonged on the other side of the grave.

Things on the television were mostly harmless when I was a child. I don't think there was a 'nine o'clock watershed' then but my parents shielded me from anything untoward until the end of the decade. This was when the BBC serialised *Quatermass and the Pit*. It was screened on Mondays from December 1958 to January 1959 (I've recently looked-up the dates and seen the serial on DVD for the first time) and it was still frightening, despite the technological crudities of the time. With an obviously far lower budget than the 'Hammer' film of a decade later, it managed to inject a genuinely eerie quality into its scenes that the film didn't recapture.

However, what I found most disturbing were the twenty minutes before episodes two to six. My practice was to go to my friend Dave's house every Monday at about six o'clock and return home by eight in time to see the week's episode. The terror I felt as I walked the half-mile through the winter streets, remembering the previous week's episode and imagining what lay ahead was almost tangible. Yet I did it, every week. I must have derived some perverse pleasure from those walks home.

Arriving home on the stroke of eight o'clock on the night when the serial was about to come to its conclusion, I decided to play a trick on my family. I opened the back door silently, very slowly creaked open that of the dining room and ushered the cat in. Behind the door, my parents and elder siblings were gathered around the television in readiness for the week's episode. It worked; they all jumped in alarm. I was pleased to find that adults could be scared, too. But I was repaid an hour later when I had to go to bed and kept glancing at my bedroom door, expecting it to be eased open by who knows what horror.

Actual death wasn't quite as far away then as it is now for most children. However, even though three boys I knew died well before my eleventh birthday (one died of Polio, one was killed in a car accident, one drowned in the local canal) I still couldn't say it was something touching me very closely. This was to change right at the end of the decade, the best part of a year after the screening of *Quatermass*.

My uncle, my father's oldest surviving brother, died. He was a widower and had lived a solitary existence in lodgings a number of miles away. His only 'outings' were to his local pub, to our house and that of another brother, also once a month on Sundays for dinner. My father announced that 'the funeral will go from here'. I asked what this meant and was told that the coffin would come to our house before it went for burial.

For no good reason, I assumed this meant the coffin would sit in our house for days. For several nights I had nightmares about this coffin, complete with its burden of my once-friendly uncle, inside our house. On two successive nights I had the most horrifying dreams I've ever had in my life. In these, the coffin, for some complex reason, had to share my bed.

In the event, I was to discover shortly before the day of the funeral that the coffin was only to be outside our house for a short time in the hearse. I didn't even see it. As the hour approached, my young cousin and I were encouraged to go out of doors 'for a short time' so we wouldn't see anything. Although we were both dressed in our best suits for the family gathering afterwards – we weren't expected to attend the actual funeral service – we seized the opportunity to get out of the house in its gloomy mood and were ready for anything. Even though was still technically forbidden for me to go to our local canal, this was what we chose to do. We walked farther along the towpath than we ever had before.

It was late in the year and the rain came down when we were a long way from home. This made the already sodden ground a morass. When we returned late in the evening, well after my cousin had been due to travel back to his home some distance away with his parents, our suits were a mess and we had a thick coating of mud on the soles and heels of our shoes.

Naturally, I didn't think this at the time – we were more concerned with the scolding we received for missing the funeral reception and with having to scrape the mud off our shoes – but now I can't help thinking this incident reflects the defiant spirit of two young boys at finding themselves young and alive on a sombre occasion.

[15] In the Playground

Tantalisingly at the fringe of my memory is a half-recollection of a day in 1954, during my primary school assembly. The headmaster (the unisex 'head teacher' came only later) informed us we would soon be able to use a newly-grassed field. This was formerly a piece of waste or common ground, sited adjacent to the classroom buildings. It would increase the playing area available to us at least fourfold.

At the time I thought little of what he said, but so important did 'The Field' become to me that I have now made a serious attempt to verify my memory. Archival resources let me down on this occasion but a human memory, now transported with its owner to California and stronger than my own on this point at least, was able to confirm what I believed.

When the day came for us to be let loose on 'The Field', we thought we were in heaven. It was nothing more than a grassed area surrounded by chain-link fencing suspended on concrete posts but we would never have believed such a prosaic description. The only thing that could be described, with a great effort of imagination, as a feature, was the short slope surrounding the field at its three boundaries with the public roads. No matter: to us the top of the slope became a castle's fortifications, the peak of a high mountain, or the High Sierras (whatever they were; we'd only heard the name in Westerns). Its five foot elevation became anything we required.

Although the area in which I lived was not a 'tough' one, most of the boys organised themselves into 'gangs', referred to by that name. Once, I discovered that a boy called Ricky Cordwainer was the named leader of a gang. I immediately attacked poor Ricky, simply because I didn't consider he was up to the task of being a gang leader.

I was the member of a 'gang' myself, but uniquely we eschewed having a leader. Three or four of us formed the nucleus of the gang and a few others drifted in and out of it as they chose. I think now this must be early evidence of anarchic streaks in us, particularly when we allowed an unpopular girl to consider herself a fringe member of our group. We defended her honour against the numerous affronts it received. The poor girl was always referred to or addressed by her surname. Her forename might as well never have existed, and she never aspired to a friendly or even teasing nickname like most of us possessed.

For football and other ball games, the boys were marched off to a local park: the girls normally had to make do for organised sport with playing netball in the main playground, skirts tucked untidily under knicker-legs. 'The Field' was our own province, except for one day a year, when School Sports Day took place upon it. Calling it by that name may be grandiloquent. It was nothing more than a few sprint races graded by age and some novelty races like the sack and egg-and-spoon. Sometimes special events were held for parents and even teachers.

Only two of the sports days stick in my mind. On the first, when I was in the infants' part of the school, I crossed the finishing line in first place in the sprint for my year. I was outraged to discover the teachers had decided my free use of elbows and disregard for lane discipline meant I should be disqualified.

A few years after this, a family of gypsy children, two girls and their older brother, became pupils at our school. Quite why they were universally known as gypsies wasn't clear to me. They lived in a house. Perhaps it was something to do with appearance and behaviour that was different. The girls wore prominent earrings and the boy a heavier gold ring in one ear. This would not be unusual now but then it was unheard of.

The boy, Joe, was a year older than me. Hearing that he was to be a competitor in one of the races, I was impressed. 'Just watch this,' I said to a group of friends. My mind was full of romantic notions about the unregarded gypsy boy proving to be fleet of foot and showing we 'Gorgias' a thing or two. In the event, he clumped across the finishing line in last place. The Wellingtons he was wearing clearly didn't help.

As I was to find out, the sun doesn't always shine in childhood, even in the summer. There were more days when permission to play on the greenery was withheld because it was damp. We weren't allowed on it at all during the winter months.

On these days, we were again confined to fairly small concreted areas on either side of the classrooms. The playground for the 5-7 year olds was segregated from those for the 8-11 year olds. It needed to be. I remember there was a huge inquest when an 8-year-old, over-exuberant with his new junior school status, crossed the divide to twist my 7-year-old arm.

There was an inquest which continued into lesson time. A hapless unknown boy with the same forename as my assailant, large for his age and with something of a bully-boy reputation, was hauled into my classroom and paraded in front of me for accusation. By this time I was getting bored with the business and was tempted to say he was the villain so as to bring a halt to the fuss. Fortunately, I didn't. This was the only lesson I ever needed that 'snitching' was something to be avoided.

Two other incidents from the infant school playground stand out in my memory. The first concerned a wooden climbing frame known by all as the 'Jungle Jim'. I liked to climb to the coveted seat on the top of the frame and take up occupation.

One day a boy, who later acquired the nickname of 'Grollie' – I think it was supposed to carry unkind hints of both 'troll' and 'ogre' - called up to me, saying I was in this throne too often and he was going to do something about it. Grollie was much bigger than me so I had visions of being hurled to the concrete below. In the event, he only climbed to the lowest level before he became distracted and lost interest in his quest.

On a later occasion, during the few minutes between my lunchtime at home and the resumption of lessons, I received some alarming news. Ann Hollister, a girl from my class, had complained to her mother about my misdemeanours. The mother had come to the school and was searching for me. In the words of my informant, she was coming to 'get me'.

I thought about this. There was no occasion I could think of when I had given offence to Ann Hollister. Could this be a case of mistaken identity? Should I stand my ground and protest my innocence? Then I saw mother and daughter, some distance away. Ann herself was not far off a foot taller than me. Her mother seemed to me like a giantess striding across the schoolyard. Ignominiously, I retreated into the boys' toilets and stayed there until well after the bell rang for the beginning of afternoon lessons.

What did the mother plan in retribution for my unknown crime? If she had found me, would I have received a verbal dressing down or something more physical? As I cowered in the boys' toilets, I was certainly assuming the latter. I stayed where I was until the coast was clear and thought I was going to receive no more than a rebuke for being late back.

I was surprised to be told by my usually lenient form teacher to 'report' my crime of unpunctuality to the head. In his office, I obligingly invented a story about not hearing the 'pips' at home because our radio had broken down. Somehow, this was accepted. Nothing further reached my ears about the Ann Hollister offence. Her mother clearly couldn't have made any complaint through official channels.

The main junior playground was, or was intended to be, for gentler games. You try telling that to a group of eight to eleven-year-old children. Yet, amidst all the rough-and-tumble, I do recall many conversations, some quite serious. We were intensely interested in things like the structure of the solar system as well as the different characteristics of various categories of cowboys and Indians.

The second junior playground, separated from the main one by a row of classrooms, was a smaller area set aside for impromptu games of football and the like. I wasn't remotely interested in these. Indeed, the only sporting activity (you could hardly dignify the annual school event with that description) I indulged in was what we called 'friendly fights'. They really did justify that description. Punching and kicking were strictly forbidden among we boys. Our activity was really no more than a kind of free-style wrestling without the acrobatics. The object was to pin the opponent's shoulders to the ground, nothing more violent. The teachers forbade the 'friendly fights' in either playground. All this did was add piquancy to the proceedings.

When I was about nine, I chanced upon the expression 'tooth and nail battle'. This greatly appealed to me. I mentioned it to a friend of mine, suggesting we should try this form of combat for ourselves. It was a serious mistake. Jack was by far the biggest boy in our year and took the term much too literally. He really did knock one of my teeth out.

Sixty and more years later, I have occasionally toyed with the idea of walking past the scenes of my primary school education. But 'Google Street View' informs me that a more modern school building has been erected on our precious playing field. To its rear, the 1935 classroom buildings, the assembly hall and the extra classroom buildings hastily thrown up after WWII have been swept away in the name of new development. I don't think I'll bother.

[16] TV Times

'Surely this silly man doesn't believe there are really horses living in that wooden box?'

Something like this was the thought running through my head as I stood with my father in the shop that morning, a sort of electrical-cum-furnishing dealer's premises about half-a-mile from our home. This was the first time I'd seen a television set and he was trying to 'kid' me into believing the race-meeting on the screen was actually taking place inside the set. I may have been only a few months past my fourth birthday but I wasn't stupid.

Nevertheless, I found the equipment not far off magical and was pleased when I realised my father intended to buy the television for what seemed to me to be, and probably was, a fantastic sum of money. I wondered if more interesting things could be seen on it than tiny horses. It wasn't long before I had the chance to find out: the set was delivered that same afternoon.

Even if you don't personally recall them, you have probably seen pictures of these old TVs with their tiny screens and huge cabinets. In our case, there was an eight-inch screen and the cabinet stood a lot taller than me. I am sure about the size of the screen because a few years afterwards there was much debate in our household as to whether we should trade up to the luxury of a massive twelve inches.

We were one of the first, if not the first, families in our road to have a television. This wasn't because we were wealthy; it came about because my father had a practical interest in things electronic, acquired in the wartime army (REME, or Royal Electrical and Mechanical Engineers). He had built a radio and what used to be called a Radiogram for the family and even a crystal set (a small radio with headphones that worked without battery or mains power) for me. Soon after this an annual treat I enjoyed used to be to accompany him to the Radio Show in Earl's Court. In one of my early visits a close circuit television was one of the exhibits. I was disappointed when I came home and my mother gave a negative response to my excited enquiry as to whether she'd seen me on television.

As more families in our neighbourhood acquired televisions, my father became the local expert on mending them. They were highly unreliable in those early years. He set up a workshop in the shed attached to our house and spent most of his free time in it. He was a television-repairer, not a television-watcher. This shed was full of things like the huge glass valves that preceded transistors (now themselves largely superseded by integrated circuits), yards of wire, screwdrivers and solder wire with flux. I loathed the smell of the last in operation.

When he was asked by friends what his younger son was going to do for a living in the adult world my father's answer was usually 'I'm trying to interest him in this'. He didn't have much success: I couldn't imagine myself spending more time amongst hot solder than I had to.

There was only one TV channel to start with. The BBC had a monopoly for its output. There wasn't to be another station until the launch of independent television in 1955 (in London; it was later elsewhere). Although our household had been pioneers with the acquisition of a television, we weren't with being two-channel viewers.

We were invited into the house next door on ITV's launch night to watch this new miracle. I recall seeing an annoying quiz programme, among other things. Most attention, adult as well as my own, was on the phenomenon of the advertisements, called 'commercials' at the time. That evening with the neighbours had a surreal feel to it because the head of the family had to work that evening and wanted the quiz programme and a few others to be recorded on his new audio tape recorder. This tape-to-tape machine (no compact discs, downloads or even cassette tapes then) was a device which had only recently become widely available. It could not be plugged into the non-existent audio socket so the only possibility was to record the programmes using a microphone. This meant we had to watch the programmes in absolute silence. I was glad to get out.

It was to be the best part of another year before we could receive ITV programmes ourselves. These came courtesy of what was called a 'converter', a device fitted to the side of the television to switch between channels.

Other add-ons came later. One was a giant magnifying glass, fitted to the front of the screen to give the illusion of seeing a bigger picture. I think I am right in saying we'd graduated to a mammoth fourteen-inch by the time of this acquisition.

The other was even dafter. This was a tri-coloured piece of Perspex, with a blue strip at the top, a yellow one in the middle, and a red one at the bottom. Viewing programmes through this contraption was supposed to give colour television. Needless to say, it wasn't a success. It does, though, show the hunger that existed at the time, particularly since colour TV was already broadcast in the USA in the nineteen-fifties. It wasn't to be seen in the UK, and then on a very limited basis, until well into the nineteen-sixties.

This is all to anticipate. Back to my first solo viewing of our eight-inch television in the spring of 1952. I can be precise about the date because this was the title of the programme coming up on the screen and I knew my father was disappointed about not being able to buy the set in time to watch the boat race after the events of the previous year, when the Oxford crew sank in the Thames. The first programme I watched called was *Paris, Spring 1952*. I assume, possibly incorrectly, that this was the title. These were in fact the first words I recall reading anywhere.

I was hypnotised by the magic revealed on the screen, although the pictures would seem clichéd enough today – the bridges across the Seine, the Eiffel Tower and so on. They entranced me. I'd heard of Paris. It was somewhere in that strange place called 'abroad', like America, where the Cowboys and Indians lived. It was to be more than another seventeen years before I saw Paris for the first time. The experience was nothing like my early television viewing or the Jerome Kearns' song. It was early winter and the place I stayed in was one of the seedier parts of Saint-Georges, itself not one of the more salubrious parts of the city. It definitely wasn't in this category in 1969, at least.

After happily watching the television for half-an-hour or so I assumed I'd be able to see it alone and as often as I liked. I was wrong. When that glorious thirty minutes of freedom (I can't remember how or why it came about) was over my viewing was to be strictly controlled and rationed. I was permitted what used to be called *Watch with Mother* but not much else. I had mixed views on the children's programmes made for children. *Rag, Tag and Bobtail*, about an unlikely friendship between a hedgehog, mouse and rabbit was something I quite liked. Another in this 'OK' category was *Hank*, a surely non-PC portrayal of the moustachioed Western hero and his arch enemy Mexican Pete 'ze bad bandit'.

The very popular *Muffin the Mule*, whose strings were originally operated by a lady called Annette Mills, left me cold. For some reason I was firmly convinced she was the sister of Freddie Mills, a light-heavyweight boxer. She wasn't. She was the sister of John Mills, the well-known actor. *Andy Pandy*, probably the best-loved children's programme of the day, used to annoy me intensely. Andy, in his striped pyjama suit, was bad enough but Teddy looked like a redundant children's toy. My greatest hostility was reserved for Looby Loo. I think she was supposed to be a rag doll who, for some reason, lived in something akin to a food hamper along with Andy and Teddy. For many years afterwards to call a girl 'Looby Loo' was the greatest insult I could confer upon her. Usually, they didn't understand. Who can blame them?

Without doubt, *Bill and Ben, the Flower Pot Men* were my favourites. One episode particularly riveted me. The string puppets explored a winter wonderland complete with frost and icicles. I was enchanted, though couldn't really tell you why. There was a minor controversy in the (adult) press about the programme in general. Someone contended that the 'flob-a-lob' speech of my heroes had a bad effect on the development of children. On behalf of Bill and Ben, I was outraged. I wanted to write to the newspaper. My mother talked me out of the idea but I wonder what the letter would have looked like.

Along with *Hank* and the unlikely-named *Mr Turnip* on a magazine programme called *Whirligig* I always looked out for a gently-spoken music presenter called Steve Race (in later years he was the presenter of a programme called *Jazz 625*). His contributions had a practical bent and afterwards I always made for our piano; these were more common in private households then than now. My father could play and, through some species of strange logic, I presumed this meant I could, too. I'd plonk away for as long as permitted.

I expect this was why the family got rid of the piano.

[17] Days Out

'Outings' were a rare occurrence during my first decade. Apart from a summer trip to the seaside on some years and frequent visits to relatives, family expeditions were uncommon enough to be memorable. I can recall most of those I had.

Visits to relatives, which my parents indulged in most Saturdays, were usually a chore. I was the youngest of my generation on both sides of my family. Of the large tribe of cousins I had, there was only one close to my own age. Apart from his sister, six years older than me and five-and-a-half his senior, nearly all the others were at least ten years older. A few had even been born during the First World War. I could hardly even think of them as belonging to my generation. Indeed, I met under a third of them.

Visits to my youngest cousin, Trevor, I did like. He lived in Wandsworth, some miles from where I lived, on the other side of the Thames. The journey to his home needed careful planning. We had to take three buses, or a combination of two buses and an underground train. This made it seem an exotic destination.   I was more than happy to make the journey as often as my parents were prepared to take me. I liked it all the more when, at the age of nine, my parents gave way to my persistent calls to allow me to travel by myself.

Once there, I'd stay overnight, for a weekend or even for a week or so during school holidays. Together Trevor and I would roam London. We liked the busiest parts of the city best, usually going to places where we could enjoy free entertainment. This wasn't because we were especially mean but because we needed every last penny of our limited funds for bus and train fares.

My special places were along various parts of the Thames. We both liked The Embankment, the area around Putney bridge and a few of the more 'touristy' spots. I don't know why this should have been, but the place resonating most with me now was far less salubrious. It was less than a mile north of my cousin's home. The uncompromisingly-named Jew's Row is still there in SW18. It's now the site of gastropubs and nearby riverside walks as well as more workaday buildings.

The place I knew was a slum street. The street gave out uncertainly onto the River Thames, muddier, dirtier and more polluted than today's waterway. Londoners at last value their great asset.

In the nineteen-fifties the lower parts of the river were declared biologically dead. I recall large, smelly mud banks and 18th century houses that looked like they should have been pulled down years before. Today, the river is clean. Well, clean-ish: I wouldn't recommend a dip in tidal waters but have swum in the river's upper reaches. The grubby area I remember has been tidied up astonishingly well. Going away from the Wandsworth area, particularly prominent in my memory for some reason is the act of the pair of escapologists whose performance we watched, open-mouthed, one day on Tower Hill. No doubt some simple trickery was involved, but I was highly impressed by the way one of them escaped from a tied sack after being bound with a combination of handcuffs, chains and rope. I almost contributed the only shilling (5p) I had to his collection. Then I remembered I'd need it to travel back to Trevor's house.

Places both of us were keen on were the London railway terminals. We travelled to most of them, though were especially fond of Victoria and Waterloo. I don't know why this should have been so: there wasn't a great deal to do for two boys with limited financial resources. It must have been that we simply enjoyed the hustle and bustle.

One day I recall in particular found Trevor and me on the concourse of Waterloo Station. We, ten years old, were playing with a machine which would punch a short message on to a thin metal strip. Not a very interesting thing to do, perhaps, but the attraction was that this enterprise would cost only a penny (0.42p). We had provided joint funding, but our inability to agree on whose name should be printed at first led to a dispute. Finally, we resolved this by compromising on a rude message. Unfortunately, or perhaps fortunately, I can't now remember what this was.

We'd begun the laborious process needed to produce it, when a man came up to us. For a moment I thought he was a representative of British Rail, whose duty was obviously to apprehend boys out for mischief. How could he have guessed our obscene intention? But he was talking in a friendly way and asking questions about the capabilities of the apparatus. Suddenly, I remembered all the parental warnings about not talking to strangers and became concerned. A glance at Trevor's wide-eyed alarm told me he was sharing my thoughts. We mumbled something and were off, leaving our incomplete obscenity in the machine.

Considering the matter later, I don't think we were in any danger. The man was very short, hardly taller than my cousin, who was big for his age. I was far shorter, but at that age what I lacked in height I made up for in stroppiness. If he did have any dark deeds in mind, he might have received a surprise. But I honestly don't think this was his intention. Not too long afterwards I formed the view that he was no more than a lonely man seeking some respite from his solitude.

About three months later, we went to Waterloo again, with the specific goal of printing a message, this time without interruption. We'd even agreed the (now forgotten) wording and had made a plan to scout the area for the man before putting our precious penny in the slot. When we reached the station, the man was nowhere to be seen. Neither was the machine.

On one occasion, my father and mother took me, together with the young boy, Paul, she looked after so his own mother could go to work, to Chiswick Empire, a survivor from the music hall days (it closed down at the end of the decade). We were to see Oliver Hardy and Stan Laurel, who were making one of their last tours of the UK.

This might have been their very last time in this country, in 1953, when Hardy was already a sick man. But I favour 1952. I do so purely because my only memories of the day are that we sat in a box, the ticket for which had been bought by my siblings as a gift for my parents and me. I was surprised to see the men wearing brown suits: I'd only seen them on a black and white screen before. Still, I do like to boast to those older than me that I've seen Laurel and Hardy live on stage.

Another parentally-escorted day I recall was when we went to Whipsnade Zoo. I remember my mother complaining about the lack of pushchairs for hire, so I must have been young. The zoo was and remains well spaced-out in the Bedfordshire countryside; walking between exhibits would have been hard on young legs. Now there is a bus service, or people can drive their own cars. At that time, far fewer families owned cars and I don't recall there being a bus service.

I probably trailed dutifully around the extensive grounds; although only recall seeing one pair of animals. They were black panthers. These creatures are actually a melanistic variety of leopard but I wasn't aware of this. They weren't actually black but a very dark brown. This colour set off their rippling muscles and gleaming emerald eyes. Incessantly, they prowled around their cage. To me, they looked huge. I suppose, in comparison to me, they were. When one of them suddenly turned and roared in our direction, I was terrified. I had nightmares that night.

Not too long after my little legs had trailed around Whipsnade Zoo came a visit to Northolt Airport, not far from my home. It was on a cloudy day, before I started school. People forget this now, but Northolt was then the UK's main airport as well as being the busiest in Europe. At that time, Heathrow was under development so this military aerodrome had been pressed into commercial use after the Second World War. Since the mid-fifties, it has been restored to the RAF, although even now it handles a number of chartered civilian flights.

Before this day, I had seen many aeroplanes, but they'd always been in the sky and some way off. They were familiar sights because my home was beneath a flight path, as it was to remain when Heathrow came into service. I was amazed to find how big the aeroplanes were: far bigger than a car, or even a bus or lorry. The ill-fated De Havilland Comet, the first commercial jet airliner, was not yet in service, so all the aircraft I saw were propeller-driven.

Of course, I had no idea of the different models. I was, though, very much taken with the triple tail plane of the Lockheed Constellation. I thought it was the smartest thing I'd ever seen. Before we left the airport, my parents bought me a bag full of tiny plastic aeroplanes, which I wasn't allowed to open until we reached home.

Immediately we did, I tore open the bag and searched for a Lockheed Constellation. There it was. The tail plane was unmistakable. Never mind that it was made of bright red plastic instead of gleaming metal. This collection of model aircraft quickly became my favourite toy, before I accumulated an impressive collection of model cowboys and Indians. I wouldn't let it out of my sight.

Where did it go?

[18] Streetwise

The only car in our road within a year of the date I started school was a brand new black Ford Popular. The Popular was one of the latest models then available.

This was owned by Mr Morris, who lived in the end house. But then, Mr Morris was always a bit different. He wore a suit and tie to work, something none of our other neighbours did. Three years later, I found out from his daughter Denise that she received 15/- (75p) weekly pocket money. She was four or five years older than me and explained she needed to buy her own clothes from that sum. It still seemed like a fortune to me.

The black Popular had been replaced by a tawny-coloured one long before any of the other neighbours bought a car. When they did, most of them first went through the intermediate stage of having what was called a 'pop-pop'. These words might mean something else now, but then they signified a small engine fixed to the back of an ordinary push bike. This propelled its owner along with all the power its name suggests. The motorised bikes moved somewhat slower than a push bike, so it seemed to me.

When cars did start to arrive, they came quickly. A variety of vehicles was parked in the street, ranging mainly from old bangers to older bangers. The mostly newer motorcycles, pride of the younger generation, were generally parked off-road. My impression was of seeing and hearing them roaring on to the road fairly infrequently. When they did it was under the disapproving gazes and 'tut-tuts' of the elders.

Our family was one of those possessing no car, so we didn't join the transport revolution. The main change for me brought about by the motor age was that it too often forced my friends and me off the road in our ball games. Not always, though. In the middle of the day there was less traffic about and, living in a Close or 'No Through Road', we could see vehicles coming and retreat no further than to the side of the road with a chorus of groans. These groans are my abiding memory of early traffic. The busy main road around the corner was an alien environment to me, even if it was one I ventured into quite frequently as the years progressed.

The first time I recall travelling inside a car myself was when I was about four. A distant relative gave my parents and me a lift in his pride and joy, a Standard Vanguard. I was impressed. The only model I'd seen before was in the form of my friend Malcolm's 'Dinky Toy' (see 22), a treasure I was always scheming to get my hands on. The relative drooled over the virtues of his car. In the event, while the car certainly gave a smooth ride, my overwhelming impression is one of the smell of petrol reaching me in the back seat.

A few years after this, I became a frequent passenger in the nineteen-thirties Vauxhall belonging to the father of my friend Jack. It might have been old-fashioned even then, but I loved this car. It took us to all sorts of places I couldn't have reached otherwise. I was very taken by its luxurious appointment, especially the amber tint to its side windows. Only recently did I discover that the coloration was due to a characteristic of the cellulose laminate used as safety glass before 1934.

When I was seven I had an altogether closer and far less pleasant encounter with a vehicle.

I'd joined 'The Commandos', the even more junior branch of the junior branch of 'The Boys Brigade', 'The Lifeboys'. This was fairly relaxed, despite its association with a church. There were few formalities of a 'junior army' type. No doubt there were prayers but, if so, they were applied lightly. The only uniform required was a navy-blue beret, adorned with a felt badge, mounted with a brass 'C'. My main memory is of playing games like cricket with an indoor ball in the Baptist church hall where we met. This was a plastic sphere with holes and wasn't supposed to break windows. It didn't, no matter how hard we tried.

'The Commandos' suited me. Every Friday evening I was happy to walk the half-mile to the church hall. For some reason I can't now recall and probably couldn't explain if I could, this was a lone project. None of my local friends went. I say 'walked', though really my locomotion was an odd combination of running, walking and skipping.

So, I was surprised one Friday evening when, skipping unconcernedly across a road half-way to the church hall, I suddenly found myself face-down, a 'Quickly' moped with spinning wheels and its rider on his back a short distance away. No doubt the accident was entirely my fault, but the moped rider was very concerned. I suppose knocking over a child would have been a serious thing. In 1955, I as a child might have feared an adult enquiry and may not have been as prepared to accept responsibility as I am in the Twenty-first Century.

Apart from skinned knees, I wasn't hurt. The 'Quickly' was powered by nothing more than a 49cc engine and its frame wasn't much heavier than that of a push bike. But, if I wasn't seriously damaged, the vehicle was a bent wreck. The rider asked if he could carry it to his home before escorting me to my own. Magnanimously, I agreed. When we reached my house, my mother was at first aghast but soon realised I wasn't really hurt and bathed my knees whilst listening to the man's version of events.

There were two consequences of this episode for me. The immediate one was good from my point of view. Before he left, the moped rider presented me with two half-crowns for not crying. I could have cried with joy. The second was less happy.

A parental conference followed and it was determined that, in future, I was not to be allowed to go to 'The Commandos' on my own. My Friday night ventures would have to be escorted. A teenage girl, the daughter of the organiser, was press-ganged into including me with the group of young charges she shepherded to the church hall. I disliked my new role as a sheep intensely. The sedate walk to the hall was frankly boring. The other boys were 'goodies' whose company I'd never have sought.

Before many weeks had passed I started to find excuses to stay away from the Commandos on a Friday and became an avid watcher of the American police series on TV called

Dragnet. I was fascinated to find the leading detective gloried in the name of 'Joe Friday' and can still remember the spoken introduction to every programme. '*The story you are about to hear is true. Only the names have been changed to protect the innocent.*' A frequent line opening the week's story began '*I was working the day watch...*' For reasons beyond my adult understanding I changed this to '*I was working the day watch in the night city*' for our street games of 'cops and robbers'. These were second in popularity only to 'cowboys and Indians'.

I doubled the size of my personal record collection (which previously had consisted of a single recording of music from the Disney cartoon *Pinocchio*) via the acquisition of a 78 rpm record of the theme music from *Dragnet*. I would play its baleful four-note introduction on the family's home-made radiogram (as they were called then) at every half-opportunity coming my way.

In short, I became an avid follower of the *Dragnet* series and was to remain one for most of the rest of the decade. But it was never as much fun as playing cricket in the Baptist church hall had been.

[19] Creatures, Mostly Small

Dogs enjoyed great freedom when I was a child. In the area of London I grew up in at least, walking leads were something seldom seen until about 1960. Unless their animals were large enough to be potentially dangerous, the usual practice was for owners to simply turf their pets out of doors in the mornings and allow them re-admission to the house only in the evenings.

We children co-existed happily with these wandering canines. Mostly, we let them be but there was one brown-and-white mongrel named Rex I particularly remember. He was very friendly and would allow anyone to pet him. All the children in my area were sad when he disappeared one day. His removal from the scene turned out to be permanent. Perhaps he'd been taken to a vet or the PDSA to be 'put down'. Or it was at least as likely he'd been run over by a car, a not infrequent occurrence at the time.

With their freedom to wander, dogs mainly deposited their excreta on the pavement. There must have been a formidable tonnage of it around. Avoiding the small mounds of ordure was an accepted hazard for pedestrians of all ages. We children took a scientific interest in the consistency of the dogs' leavings. Particularly valued sightings were of the 'whites'. I now assume the excrement came in that colour because of the dogs' encounters with worming powder, although none of my age group guessed this at the time. To us, it was a simple miracle of nature.

Until the rules of pet ownership started to change a few years later, and the use of leads became more common, our family had no dog. When I was very young, we had a cat. Its name was Blackie. I never did know what sex it was. I was as indifferent to this animal as he or she was to me. It did nothing all day apart from sleep in various places around the house. Now, I suppose the creature might have led an especially exotic night life, although of course this wasn't an observation I made at the time. It was always sleeping when I got up and when I went to bed.

One day, whitish patches started to appear in its black fur. My mother took unsuspecting Blackie to the PDSA, where it was destroyed. She announced that the vet had said the cat had 'distemper' and would have to be 'put to sleep'. For years afterward I thought this was a reference to an actual disease and would tell the other children 'we had a cat but it died of distemper'. I formed improbable images of this disease: 'distemper' was also the name used at the time for ceiling whitewash. I imagined the black cat turning gradually white and wondered why my mother hadn't kept the cat for me to witness the phenomenon.

Later, I overheard her telling my father that the cat had to go 'because there were young children in the house'. There is in fact a specific, though uncommon, viral disease called Feline Panleukopenia, but this cannot be transmitted to humans. I don't think 'Blackie' really had this illness. The creature was probably generally unwell and was unlucky enough to share a house with a small child.

Before the decade was out, the family had a more interesting cat: it could sit up and beg like a dog. My mother had a succession of four budgerigars and I even owned a scamp of a dog myself. But my real interest lay in creatures of the wild.

'Proper' wildlife was not a common sight in my urban environment and my hands-on experience was confined to things like newts, frogs, and slow-worms. I had therefore to scale down my ambitions.

This was no real problem. Insects were in plentiful supply – we now know there really were many more small creatures around in those days, so it wasn't simply a case of me living my life nearer to their altitude. I could recognise numerous types of beetle (if not by their proper names); I discovered caterpillars miraculously transformed into butterflies and spent much time in constructing not altogether secure breeding batteries. If any of the local children discovered an unrecognised species I would be consulted as to what it was. If I didn't know what it was then I was more than happy to oblige by making up a suitable name.

Every inch of our garden was familiar to me. I knew exactly where to find each one of the considerable number of ants' nests it held and even drew a map identifying the various species. To me, these were confined to the common black; the stinging red and the exotic yellow. By dint of experimentation I found that the common black was the toughest: I was surprised to find that any red ant, despite its sting, would be quickly assassinated if it were dropped into a nest of blacks or yellows, whereas a black or yellow ant would often escape from a hostile colony.

Autumn was a good time. Numerous Crane Flies (usually, along with Harvestmen, called 'Daddy Long Legs') would hatch in the damp grass. With their slow, clumsy flight, these could easily be caught by hand. Once, in my primary school, I caught a clutch of four on the edge of the playing field and quietly released them in my classroom.

To her credit, although her near-hysteria was evident, my teacher kept her emotions under control. To their credit, the few boys who were in on my secret kept it to themselves and, despite some suspicious looks from the teacher and outright accusations from some of the girls, my misdeed went unpunished.

My absolute favourites from the world of insects were the grasshoppers. In the summer, especially on the hottest days before the depredations of chemical treatments did their worst, their stridulations (the noise made by rubbing limbs together) could be very loud to young ears close to the ground. These would lead small hands unfailingly to a quarry which provided altogether more of a challenge than the one provided by comical crane flies. If your hand didn't close upon the small creatures quickly enough their strong back legs would enable them to leap a few feet away. If you were successful in grasping one, you could feel its powerful hindquarters flicking against your palm.

What I liked most about grasshoppers were their small, neat faces. To me, these spoke of intelligence. Surely these animals couldn't be of the same order as ants and beetles? I developed all sorts of fantasies about them. I imagined them to be tiny aliens who lived among us.

Towards the end of the decade, by which time my hands-on variety of entomology had mainly ceased, there was a television serial called *Quatermass and the Pit* [see 14] I found it the most gripping, terrifying thing I'd seen on a screen, before or since. When the corpses of aliens (who'd emanated from Mars) were revealed, they proved to be nothing less than Devilish giant grasshoppers.

The writer, Nigel Kneale, must also have possessed an overblown imagination.

[20] Number Thirty-one

Number thirty-one (like number thirty-four – see [22]) didn't really have that number. The road where I grew up had only twenty-seven houses. But I wanted to use a pseudonym for the house as well as for the members of the two families who lived in it during the nineteen-fifties.

Like the road it was in, the house was unexceptional in any way. I don't want to stoop to the condescension of 'typical'. I've chosen the house more or less at random.

Anyway, it's the people who lived in the house I really want to write about. The first family I can remember living there were the Hodges. They were a family of five. The father was a dumpy, worried-looking man. Later, I found out he had things to worry about. Like most of the adult males I remember from the time, he spoke seldom or never in my hearing.

Perhaps this was an after-effect of the terrible war every one of the adults around us had been through. Naturally, this wasn't an observation I made at the time: back then I merely accepted it as part of the normal pattern of things: adult males, or 'Dads' as most of those of the previous generation I knew actually were, simply didn't speak.

Mrs Hodge was a smart, attractive woman with a dreamy look in her blue eyes. 'Attractive' is a word I'm using with the benefit of more mature vision turned upon the image I have retained in my memory. At the time I was merely aware that she looked younger than most of the 'Mums' I knew. Unusually for the time, she had a full-time job.

Her eldest child was a daughter, Belinda. She was about twelve when I first knew her, a very good-looking girl: even to my seven-year-old eye she was the image of her mother. Mrs Hodge had two sons. One of them was Don, three years older than me. I knew him well. A large part of this piece is concerned with him.

I didn't know whether the other son was older or younger, nor did I ever find out his name. Indeed, I wouldn't even have known of his existence if my mother hadn't told me of him. He was 'strange' in some undefined way, spending the whole of each day closeted in a bedroom. This had locks fitted to the windows: apparently on one occasion he had frightened his family and neighbours when breaking both wrists by leaping out of the window to the lawn below.

This locking-up was the sum total of his specialist care at home, as far as I was aware. Looking back, I suppose he might have gone away to a 'special school' somewhere, although I had no knowledge of this at the time. Occasionally, I went into number thirty-one while Don and Belinda were performing their allotted household chores before Mrs Hodge arrived home from work. These were vaguely exotic rites to me, and I was always pleased to be allowed in to witness them. But, after I learned of the second son's existence, I was uncomfortably aware of the unseen presence upstairs and was reluctant to go into the house.

Don's pride and joy was his soap-box cart. These odd devices, apparently known by strange names like 'gambos' in other parts of the country, were already going out of fashion by the nineteen fifties, but they still had an existence outside the pages of comics. My only real experience with one was with the vehicle built and owned by Don.

The 'soap-box' name was derived from the 'body', which I suppose at one time was often a wooden soap-box. This was bolted roughly to a wooden 'chassis', onto which were fitted four wheels, two at the back and two at the front. The front wheels were attached to a bogie-plank to give articulation. All four wheels were usually taken from old prams: ideally the back-wheels would be larger than the bogie-wheels. Steering could be achieved by the simple device of a piece of string attached to the bogie-plank, but boys used to regard it as point of honour to incorporate a steering wheel of some kind into the often elaborate mechanisms, even if the result of their engineering efforts was to make the cart next to impossible to steer. Some carts, though not Don's, even had a braking-mechanism.

One thing no soap-box cart had was any kind of motive power. Unless the course was downhill, this would be provided by a (usually smaller) boy. In Don's case, the smaller boy was nearly always me. I don't ever remember being allowed to be the driver. 'When you're a bit older,' I was always told. This, of course, was Don's reason for befriending a boy who was so much younger. It took me a few years to realise it.

My final appreciation of my status came when I witnessed a conversation between Don and a boy of his own age. 'I get all the little kids around here to push me,' he boasted. 'All the little kids' essentially meant me.

Shortly after this I was, as usual, in my appointed place behind Don's soap-box cart. Our route took us across a road, and I stopped to let a milk float pass. Don hectored me about my hesitant ways, saying that milk floats travelled slowly and we could easily have made it across. I wasn't so sure. Anyway, I had cause for caution; just the week before I had been spread-eagled in the middle of a road by a moped (see [18]) which I had clearly expected to get out of my way rather than vice-versa.

These two events combined to make me see Don in a different light. But still, for the short remaining time I knew him, I continued to push the cart without major complaint. I have often wondered why.

Then Mrs Hodge, Belinda and Don started to go for Sunday bike-rides with a grey-haired man who was the mother's boss in work. Don excitedly told me this worthy provided all three bikes, and described how on one of the cycle rides a lightning-bolt struck very close to them.

This arrangement continued for several weeks. Mr Hodge wasn't mentioned at all. Then, one day, I knocked on the door of number thirty-one and had no answer. Eventually, I discovered Mrs Hodge had decamped with the grey-haired man, Belinda and Don. Mr Hodge soon afterwards disappeared to a place unknown. I often wonder where the mysterious boy upstairs went.

For a short while number thirty-one remained empty. Then, there came a new family, the Hoopers. There were three children: John, a boy of my own age; Paul, a year younger; and Hannah, a daughter who was even younger and so beneath my notice.

Both of the boys became my friends. John, a few years later, even tried to seek my collaboration on his mathematics homework. This must have been an act of desperation on his part. I was the last person whose help he should have tried to enlist with anything vaguely numeric.

Mr Hooper kept tropical fish, a few years before the hobby exploded in popularity. Later, when it was in full swing, we even had a tank at home ourselves.

In many ways, Mrs Hooper was the most interesting member of the family, although I didn't realise this at the time. She was invariably referred to (not to her face) as 'The German Woman'. What must it have been like, to be a native of a country we had been at war with a dozen years before?

This was not a thought I had at the time. But this question causes me to seriously ponder as an adult. She may not have been a German at all. She may have been a civilian in some other Central or East European nation – perhaps she was really a Czech or Pole, or a former citizen of some other faraway country of which we knew nothing.

[21] Gone Fishin'

In the June before my tenth birthday, I received permission to go fishing in the canal at the end of my road. For the first year or two, my authorised fishing trips had to be in the company of my elder brother. The canal, or 'cut' as it was more often called, was a forbidden place. In fact, it was the only local feature definitely off limits to me.

In my younger days, a few children, one a friend of mine, had drowned in its none-too-deep but murky waters. There were dark stories of child-stealing gypsies and 'strange men'. The latter would do unspecified but horrific things to you. I never found any evidence of either of these phenomena, but the stories, more so than the adult prohibition, were enough to keep me away from the canal and the piece of waste ground we all called 'The Dump' through which it flowed. At least, they were enough kept me away for most of the time.

So, my graduation to the status of semi-authorised fisherman was like being issued with a passport to some exotic land. The rod I first used was not the traditional wispy cane thing, but a heavy steel object. Adults called it a 'tank aerial' and its origins may indeed have been as a piece of war surplus, as definitely was the gas mask bag I used to carry my meagre angling equipment to the canal.

My fishing-tackle consisted of nothing more than the essentials: line on a second-hand reel I had scrounged from somewhere, two floats, lead weights in a tiny steel box and a few hooks. A landing and 'keep' net, a rod rest, a fishing stool and all the items with which the adult coarse angler burdened himself (it was always a 'him') were seen by me as being impossible luxuries.

My first fishing trip was on a Sunday afternoon, probably the most unproductive time of the week. This was nothing to do with piscine Sunday Services and not much to do with those aimed at their human hunters. It was often too warm in the summer for fish to feed during the middle of the day and there was stiff competition for the better angling marks. But, in those days, I was still required to attend Sunday school and had to endure this and the even more onerous duty of Sunday dinner before I was permitted the frivolity of fishing.

Even if I say it myself, I was a model angler. I held the heavy rod perfectly still, never letting it out of my hands for a moment, concentrating intently on the yellow or red plastic quill floating in the mainly still water. None of the fooling around throwing 'darts' (from the weeds more properly called 'green foxtails', but we didn't know this) or the various activities most other junior anglers indulged in. I wanted to be ready for my fish.

I couldn't afford maggots, the recommended bait. These were called 'gentles' by the fishing community for some unknown reason. Goodness knows why they received this sobriquet; the writhing mass of maggots in a plastic bait box was anything but gentle. I simply used bread paste, made quickly and easily by tearing the crust from a slice of the putty-like white bread unaccountably popular at the time, adding a few drops of water, and kneading the result for a few minutes.

The fish seemed to like it and I rarely had recourse to maggots thereafter. I even spurned the cheese and hempseed reputed to attract Roach, the favoured catch of the elder statesmen of the canal, whist being ignored by the lesser breed I made my quarry for the first year or two. So, on that Sunday afternoon, I was ready for my fish.

And, on that first day by the water, they obliged. There were three of them, all Gudgeon. These are small, delicate creatures, rarely more than four inches long, with barbules beneath their mouths. Older anglers poured scorn on these tiddlers, preferring the bright silver Roach, the other main species stocked in the canal. Many of these were hardly bigger than the Gudgeon but, if you were very lucky, there were Roach of a pound or two to be caught.

The day fishing permits, of which I only ever bought a handful, listed every variety of coarse fish, but the only other species I ever saw in the fourteen or so years I fished in the canal were a few Perch. Those day tickets were something of a joke. Word would go along the towpath that 'the bailiff's coming' and immediately the young boys, and many of the not-so-young boys, would hide their rods and other equipment in the undergrowth to avoid paying the one shilling (5p) for a day ticket. The bailiff seemed to conspire in this farce. At least, I never saw one enquire as to why so many boys were standing on the canal bank, vacantly staring into the water.

I must have gone fishing in the canal on at least three occasions a week on average, for the years I used the canal. The best times of all were the June evenings when the light allowed you to fish until around ten o'clock. There was something magical about fishing on a late midsummer evening. Even the clouds of midges swarming around your head were part of the charm. The still waters would tempt you into making 'one more cast' after another, until screwing your eyes up in the semi-darkness no longer brought sight of the brightly painted float.

At that time, the canal was still a working transport system, with fairly frequent narrow-boats (we called them 'barges') to be seen. There were no pleasure craft then. No doubt the colourful working vessels were an attractive sight, but we hated them. They churned up our beloved water and made fishing impossible for fifteen minutes or so. Worst of all, from our point of view, were the smaller number of horse-drawn craft. These not only brought all the problems of the motorised vessels but, into the bargain, the towpath had to be cleared of tackle and ourselves to let the horses pass.

Later, I fished more seriously in the River Thames and other waters, including the sea and fast-flowing trout rivers. I greatly extended my quarry, both in terms of the size and number of species I caught. Like more earnest fishermen I surrounded myself with all kinds of tackle. I even turned my hand to making copper or aluminium 'spoons' or spinners for catching pike.

In time, the humble Gudgeon became something to be avoided in these grander waters. But it is still the evenings by the dirty old canal I remember best.

[22] Number Thirty-four

The first family I remember living in Number Thirty-four were the Burtons. My memory of Mr Burton is of a quite elderly (so it seemed to me) man who spoke not at all to my recollection. In contrast, Mrs Burton had a great deal to say for herself. She always seemed to be shouting at her eldest son, Malcolm, an amiable boy some years older than me and far taller.

Malcolm had three sisters, all younger than himself. One of them may even have been slightly older than me but, to be honest, even though I was friendly with a number of other girls in the street and, looking back, can claim not to have been a young male chauvinist, I didn't pay this trio much attention.

My friend was the owner of three very battered 'Dinky Toy' cars, a Standard Vanguard, an Austin Seven and a Riley of ancient appearance. Whether Malcolm or one of his sisters had experimentally daubed them with green and black paint, I couldn't say, but the uniform finish on the toy cars was anything but pristine. What I did like about these cars was that they were incredibly smooth-running. Perhaps an experimental oil-can had been at work.

I'd happily let Malcolm borrow my two comparatively gleaming toy cars, a red Austin Somerset and mustard-coloured Hillman Minx, in exchange for the opportunity to push his own vehicles around the road system we scrawled on the pavement in front of my house. Only about seven or so years before the road had been farmland and for some reason there was plenty of chalk left to be found near the surface of the topsoil by we young highway engineers. We always seemed to be playing with the cars. In fact I don't recall us ever playing anything else together. Perhaps we didn't.

One day we had some sort of disagreement, which quickly became physical. I wrestled Malcolm to the ground. This was very easy to do: although he was taller and older than me, he had no clue when it came to the techniques of boyish fighting. He ran up the street to his own house, sobbing.

A few minutes later he emerged, apprehensive determination written on his features. His mother had told him, he informed me, that I was only a shrimp and he should come back and teach me a lesson. She hadn't given him any wrestling coaching, though, because our brief encounter ended in the same way, with Malcolm picking himself up from the ground and running home, crying.

It horrified me when, a few minutes later, he once again came out of his house, tears streaming down his face, marching toward me. This time he didn't say anything, but his mother had clearly sent him out again. Even at the time I couldn't have said exactly what our original dispute was about, so it was with some reluctance I pushed him to the ground once more.

I feared to sustain the exercise any longer and so on this occasion, when he ran into his house, I hid in a neighbour's garden for half-an-hour. Friends later told me that Malcolm had indeed come looking for me, so in a way you could say he won the war through his dogged and tearful persistence, even though he didn't win any of its battles. Fortunately the next day, after some initial frostiness, we resumed our traffic game.

The Burtons moved away when I was about eight and the Perry family took their place. The head of the household was a non-talkative but cheerful Irishman. His wife, according to my mother, was a Londoner. The important thing for me was that they had a son of around my own age (actually, he was several months younger). Like Malcolm, Michael had three sisters. In his case one of them, Penny, was older. I think in age I came somewhere mid-way between brother and sister.

Michael was an intelligent boy and we used to have long, earnest conversations about every subject under the Sun. He sometimes had some ideas that puzzled me, though. The family were Catholic, which to me meant nothing more than the fact that he went to a different school. Many children, including me, were confined to barracks for whole swathes of each Sunday. My family also made a practice of eating fish on Friday and I knew we weren't Catholics. The Perrys, especially Michael, were very conscious of their religion. One day, my friend amazed me by telling me I had always to obey the Queen so it was better to be a Catholic. He was and so had only to obey the Pope. I couldn't imagine either the Queen or the Pope sparing the time to come around to tell us what to do.

Once we were having one of our deep conversations on my back porch when a group of girls, including Michael's two younger sisters, came through the gate to ask if they could look at the pond in our back garden. I agreed and we returned to talking. Minutes later, the girls returned. The youngest sister, a girl of about five or six called Leslie, was wailing loudly. It seemed she'd fallen into the pond and had been rescued by the others. Michael turned not a hair. We'd have resumed our debate but I wanted to ensure the goldfish hadn't been harmed.

Mrs Perry kept her four children on a tight rein. It amused me, used to roving far and wide, to try to trick Michael into stepping beyond his permitted bounds, the outpost of which was marked by the 'No Through Road' sign at the start of our road.

She was a good sport, Mrs Perry. I liked her and for some reason she approved of Michael taking me as a friend, even though she looked down upon many of the other local boys. On one occasion she permitted me to use a half-full box of indoor fireworks in her best room. I had obtained these through some probably doubtful trading deal with another boy. All four of the Perry children were very taken with this unaccustomed spectacular.

An interest Michael and I shared was in the building of plastic model aircraft. Our approaches were rather different. He would take extreme care over every aspect of the construction. There was never any excess glue (for some reason called cement) on his transparent cockpit windows and all the parts that should have moved in his few more expensive models really did move. He even painted his aeroplanes and insisted the paint should be allowed to dry before they could be taken on a mission.

In contrast, for me construction was a necessary evil to be got out of the way as quickly as possible. Painting was a frivolity only delaying the real purpose of model-making, which was to strengthen our combined air forces so they could do battle with that of Sumeria.

The Sumerian Air Force was owned and maintained by Terry, a neighbour of ours. Michael had somehow persuaded Terry that his collection represented the Evil Empire of Sumeria and thus he was required to lose all the aerial conflicts with the 'good' allies (Michael and me). This suited me; I liked to be on the winning side. Sumeria in fact, was an ancient and distinguished civilisation in what is now Southern Iraq and one of the first to employ writing.

Never mind about history, though. Michael managed to make the word 'Sumeria' represent all that is dark in the world. It always surprised me when Terry at least half-accepted the ignoble part he was required to play and still flew out his aeroplanes as often as we required. He had more pocket-money than we did and so there were more frequent additions to the Sumerian Air Force. It made no difference to the country's military prowess.

Playing in the Perry home in the evenings was something I often enjoyed. This was not least because they had no television set to interfere with the process. We took part in what was almost a children's club, with the four oldest of us participating (poor Leslie was usually deemed by all to be too young and so was relegated to the role of audience for the short time before she was banished to bed). Mrs Perry acted as organiser/referee/peacemaker.

The games were normally of the old-fashioned parlour game style, like Consequences and Charades, but sometimes we were permitted to roam over the darkened house with torches indulging in Hide-and-Seek, Sardines and other adventures whose names I now forget.

There was one evening when Mrs Perry might have regretted her liberal stance as Gamesmaster for number thirty-four. We were playing 'Alibis'. In this the object of the game was for two of the players to concoct an alibi for the time when a supposed crime was committed. The others had the task of interrogating them to see if they could find any conflicts in what was said.

Penny and I were to be the alibi-makers in this particular game. As required, we went into another room and, when we were satisfied that our alibi was strong, we returned to be interviewed.

To every question, our answer was 'we were in bed!'

The others were thrown by our novel and perhaps unfair approach. Mrs Perry looked uncomfortable. Eventually one of the opposing children (I think the second daughter, Catherine) demanded to know if we were in bed together the whole time.

'Yes!' we both said.

'Oo, no', murmured Mrs Perry.

'Yes!' we insisted.

Our answers were given in total innocence. I was vaguely aware there was something dubious about our alibi, but unsure as to quite what or why. Anyway, virtue has its reward. We won the game.

[23] Hair

In early 1970, I went to see the rock musical *Hair*. The anti-establishment, Vietnam-protesting production came in many ways to define the counter-culture of the later nineteen-sixties. Indeed, my companion complained we were already too late to get the best out of seeing the musical. She maintained we should have gone to see it a few years earlier, when it was *the* talking point of London. In fact, I'd only met her a month or two before.

To me, the performance had a different resonance. It reminded me of my childhood. The writers of the musical were older than me, but most of the cast and audience were of around my age. They'd have seen the *Hair* of the title as a badge of progressive thinking. The long hair of the young 'goodies' in the cast sanctified them. In their hostile world, they were surrounded by short-haired demons whose main purpose was to make sure they conformed by being sent meekly to war and, as an essential part of this process, were shorn of their glory.

Being conscripted for military service was fortunately not a personal problem for us in the UK at that time but is it too fanciful to say the way I felt about my precious hair in the nineteen-fifties made me instinctively side with the young protestors? Personally, I don't think it is.

The Sundays on which I was due to have my hair trimmed were the worst part of what I remember of my least favourite day. I was required to sit miserably on a stool perched atop a wooden chair. Then, whilst I was rocking precariously to the accompaniment of his anguished cries of 'sit still', my father would cut my hair with some ancient hair clippers. Until later in the decade, when he acquired an electric trimmer, these were manually operated. No doubt they were of pre-war origin. In practice this meant that, every so often, the trimmers would baulk at their task and give me an almighty pinch instead of lopping off a lock of hair. I hated it. No wonder so many males of my generation grew their hair long as soon as they could.

Subjectively, it feels as if my 'trims' were a weekly occurrence, though of course this couldn't have been the case. My father must have disliked giving me haircuts as much as I disliked receiving them. At all events, he eventually relented and let me have my hair done by a hairdresser.

And he was a hairdresser, too. His 'salon' was in the middle of the block of shops around the corner from us, and he was called 'Jacques'. It sounds French but in fact the owner was a Cypriot. Whether it was a name assumed for hairdressing purposes I don't know but he was known by all under that name. Jacques had fled his homeland as a result of the 'Enosis' troubles of the mid nineteen-fifties. I don't know whether he was of Greek or Turkish ethnicity but I do recall hearing him telling an adult customer he was 'never going back'.

The shop window carried photographs of men and women with sleek hair in the latest styles. In the case of men, lashings of Brylcreem, a white slimy substance, were used to hold the waves in place. It seemed especially disgusting stuff to me at the time. This was probably because we always had a jar of it at home, as did most families. It was plastered on my hair whenever we were to go somewhere special.

Dennis Compton, the cricketer and at one stage the number one hero of mine, was the 'face' of the early TV advertisements. The company also used jingles with the words 'a little dab'll do yer' and 'they love to get their fingers in your hair'. The latter was widely mocked; as well it deserved to be.

I used to have serious debates with myself as to whether it would be worth enduring the Brylcreem if I could wear my hair as long as the men in the photographs. This question was purely hypothetical, of course. The important thing was that the hairdressers in Jacques salon would take as much or as little hair off as you asked. Naturally, my preferences were minimalist. I got away with it twice but then was firmly told that I'd have to go to a 'proper barber'. There was such a 'proper barber' half-a-mile down the road. It was called 'Phil's' and his shop was stark and bare in comparison with Jacques' establishment. No matter what style we asked for, Phil or one of his assistants would give us a severe short-back-and-sides. This suited my parents but not me.

Two or three months after ceasing to be a customer of Jacques, I met a young man I knew slightly, a teenager I suppose he was, and spoke to him and his friend in a shop doorway. He wore all the 'Teddy Boy' regalia, light blue suit with drainpipe trousers, yellow shirt, suede shoes and bootlace tie. Most importantly he carried a comb, which he flicked lovingly and frequently through his hair.

I can't remember the detail of what was said, but do remember him telling me I should go back to Jacques and 'get a proper DA like me'. I had no idea what DA stood for so asked if it stood for 'District Attorney'. 'That's right,' he said, turning to his friend and laughing. 'Go and tell your Mum.' In fact the initials stood for 'duck's arse'.

Towards the end of the decade, my sister Mary, aided and abetted by my mother, went through a period of 'doing my hair' before I went to my primary school. This involved combing and brushing it into a coif. They went into ecstasies about this coif, but I used to hate it in my soul. I'd preserve it until I walked to the end of my street. Then, as soon as I was near to the corner and thought I was safely out of sight, I'd furiously hand-brush it forward into what I thought was more like a boy's hair should be. Years later, my mother and sister told me they often laughingly watched my attempts at manual coiffure.

What I thought was a boy's hairstyle was probably in reality an utter mess, but there was a positive aspect to this episode. The competing attentions to my hair resulted in an unusual kind of style, with a loose parting in the middle and two waves falling down gracefully over my forehead. If I could, I'd style my hair in a similar way now. But I can't. Male pattern baldness set in when I was in my twenties!

[24] 1957 And All That

Our wooden radio – they were called wirelesses then but all the same were full of wires and huge glass objects called valves – gave out a 'beep, beep' sound. My friend and I listened intently. It was a tinny, unreal noise but it was the most important one of the Twentieth Century. This was October, 1957 and we were hearing a recording of *Sputnik I* in its orbit around the Earth.

For reasons I can't now explain, we'd illuminated the room using only the coloured beams of two torches shining upwards on our faces to give a spooky effect. Green was the favoured colour. Perhaps we thought this would enhance the drama of the occasion.

Michael Perry's dark eyes glittered eagerly in the torchlight and we both knew we were hearing something very special. What puzzled us most was this history was being made by the dark empire of the Soviet Union. At that time the nation was regarded with real fear by most people in these islands. The vast Russian lands might as well have been inhabited by a race of ogres.

One of our regular discussions concerned Michael's belief that our Government was condoning the flight of Russian bombers over our houses at night. We lived beneath a Heathrow flight path. This I thought to be a more likely explanation for the aeroplanes we could hear flying above. Nevertheless, I was at the same time half-convinced of the accuracy of my friend's opinion.

Despite the oddity of his views on this particular subject, I understand with the benefit of adult reflection, that Michael was, generally speaking, a horribly mature and insightful not quite ten-year-old. I suppose I was one myself. We knew without saying a word as we listened to the radio broadcast that we would discuss what had happened many times over the coming weeks and months. And so we did.

Our discussions, though, did not match the reality of what was to take place over the next twelve years. Less than a month after the launch of *Sputnik I*, a dog, Laika, became the first living creature – the animal was alive at the time of the launch, at least – to go into space. In January, 1959, *Lunik I* became the first satellite to travel beyond a gravity that had kept everything and everybody imprisoned on our planet for billions of years. The following September saw its sister rocket, *Lunik II*, crash-landing on The Moon. In the next month *Lunik III* shattered a few myths by sending back photographs of the hitherto unseen far side of The Moon. It could be only a matter of time before manned flights became a reality. We did not have to wait long. Yugi Gagarin made history on 12 April, 1961, after a brief voyage into space.

Meanwhile the Americans were becoming frantic at the way in which their rivals for world leadership were forging ahead. Soon, they were pouring many more dollars into research than the Russians could muster in roubles. Alan Shepherd made the first American manned spaceflight in May, 1961. This was weeks after Gagarin's flight. A few days after this the first of the new betting shops were opened in the UK. By then, no-one could have found odds against the might of the dollar being the eventual winner of the Space Race.

Over the next eight years dollars and roubles were spent at a fantastic rate to achieve what had been the politicians' aim since 1957: the first landing on and the safe return from The Moon. When Neil Armstrong made his 'one small step for man; one giant leap for mankind' on our only natural satellite, it was only 21st July 1969, fewer than twelve years after Michael and I had heard *Sputnik I* on the radio.

This was a remarkable achievement; surely one of the greatest in the story of mankind. By 1969 I had lost contact with Michael. If I hadn't, we would have been sure to speculate on Mankind's first voyage to Mars. At this time such a thing was widely and realistically expected within another twelve years. No doubt unmanned landings would have been made on a few comets and the more distant outer planets along the way. Interstellar voyages would have become more than an idle dream.

*

None of this was to be. The politicians decided America had 'won' the Space Race. They lost interest in all that expensive, if productive, research. The world turned in on itself and new priorities were found. These were mainly to do with giving the appearance of increasing the material wealth of the privileged quarter or third of the Earth's population. Any thoughts of the advancement of mankind – which may have been no more than incidental in the first place – were quietly shelved

Today, we reap the 'rewards' of this failure of nerve. As the overworked man uses his mobile telephone to call his wife or partner to explain he will be late home again because of the crumbling and congested public transport system, perhaps he'll begin to realise he will not find the time tonight to stroke the Persian Cat or kick the Afghan Hound. Maybe he will also spare a few minutes to think of what might have been if events had unfolded differently and more visionary priorities had been followed in the final third of the last century.

Or perhaps mine is a jaundiced view. Even as I write there may be two horribly mature and insightful not quite ten-year-olds listening to the radio, or more likely exchanging emails or tweeting about something they have discovered on the Internet. Perhaps this will lead to the breaking of the iron chains with which our species has chosen to fetter itself. Perhaps.

[25] The Sickie Vickie

Does anyone collect postage stamps these days?

Of course they must do. But they would be mainly adults with serious philatelic intent or else small boys attracted by the miniature pictures. In the nineteen-fifties, a large proportion of boys (but few girls, so it seemed from my casual observations) indulged in the hobby. From the ages of about seven to twelve or thirteen I was a collector myself.

My somewhat obsessive interest in stamps began when Jack, a veteran collector of my own age, showed me his collection. This was already impressive for one so young. His mother suggested I should also take up the hobby and he gave me a fair number of his duplicates. I bought a stamp album and a packet of hinges (no-one applied messier adhesives to their precious bits of paper) and I was off.

From the outset, Jack and I were extraordinarily competitive about our stamps. I made an encouraging start by buying a 'Hunter' stamp album (named after the 'Hawker Hunter' jet fighter aeroplane, at the time newly in service with the RAF). At the cost of one shilling (5p) it put the opposing sixpenny (2½p) 'Blue Lagoon' album into the shade. After this first flourish, though, I never quite caught up, save for a precious few months in 1958.

We were very serious about our charges, and scornful of the "pretty pictures' school of philately. What I mean by this is that, by this time, many countries were becoming increasingly aware of the revenues to be elicited from enthusiasts attracted by the pictorial qualities of their postage stamps. Governments therefore sought to gain income simply by producing large numbers of new issues. These became more important for their decorative qualities than postal use.

This wasn't the situation in the United Kingdom of the nineteen-fifties. From the time postage stamps were first issued in 1840 to the time I started collecting, there had been a frugal dozen 'commemorative sets' issued. The stamps in this country were firmly for postal purposes. 'Sets' only occurred as a by-product of the necessity of having a range of different values, differentiated by colour as well as by the inscription on the stamp. Variations in design were of minor importance. When we held a British stamp (with tweezers, not in the hand, we were too respectful for any such thing) we could be sure we were looking upon a genuine official label that had seen proper service attached to a letter or parcel.

It was inevitable that two boys with these austere views should hold that the stamps of our nation must be somehow 'superior' to the rest and accord them special reverence. Nothing gave us greater pleasure than to discover a new (to us) specimen in one of the threepenny or sixpenny miscellaneous packets sold by 'H. Always', a corner tobacconist and sweetshop in our town centre.

We would spend as much time as we were permitted gazing longingly at these packets, wondering if the corner of a stamp we could glimpse at the back of a packet could be an undiscovered treasure. Once, Mr Always told us to keep our grubby hands away from the stamps. When we protested that our hands were clean, he informed us that 'little boys' hands are always grubby'. We couldn't think of an answer to that.

A couple of years after I'd joined the fraternity, a ½d stamp from the 'Jubilee Issue' of Queen Victoria came into my friend's possession. This set of stamps wasn't really issued to commemorate anything, but it first appeared in 1887, the year of the Queen's Golden Jubilee, and the name stuck. Ecstatic, he showed it to an older boy in the neighbourhood, who confidently announced that 'it would be worth anything between £2 and £350'. We soon discovered it was not worth a fraction of even the lower figure. Even today, it would be valued in pence rather than pounds.

No matter; I was insanely envious. My friend had beaten me to the acquisition of the first Victorian stamp. We were both to obtain other low-valued stamps from the 'Jubilee Issue' and even a few older specimens, but by this time we knew enough, even before taking the obligatory peek inside the Bible of philatelists, the Stanley Gibbons Postage Stamp Catalogue, to realise none of them was worth much. Secretly, or perhaps not-so-secretly, I believed that, in the interests of justice, the next notable discovery should be mine.

When I was ten years old, I was sure such a find had fallen into my lap.

I was in the house of Ronnie, the boy next door, when it happened. We were playing with his train set. Knowing my interest in stamps, he showed me his own album. He wasn't a serious collector; in fact most of his collection had been assembled by an uncle years before. I'm sure Ronnie was acting from amused tolerance; I was a frequent borrower of his copy of a 'White's Postage Stamp Catalogue' from 1950 that had come into his possession from the same uncle.

He, no doubt, was keen to resume the serious business of playing with the train set laid out on the floor. But the album fascinated me and I was reluctant to put it down. It was at least thirty years old and had clearly in years past housed a fine collection. Now, many of the pages consisted largely of the shrivelled corpses of ancient stamp hinges. It didn't need detective skills of a high order to realise the more valuable stamps had been removed at some time in the past. As I leafed through the pages, I wondered what treasures they had once borne. Then, I saw it.

It was an 1865 sixpenny lilac postage stamp. Although something of such high denomination would probably have been used on a small parcel, it wasn't too badly obliterated by the postmark, in accordance with the usual practice of that era. I was aware that in 1865, the UK had a Liberal Government in power and that *Alice's Adventures in Wonderland* had been published. I knew this was also the year the American Civil War, a key event on my horizon, ended. My brand of philately promoted a feeling for history and geography.

Here, in my hands, I held a tangible piece of that history. The parcel the stamp once adorned might have been posted by Lewis Carroll himself. I had to have it. Although I was normally a canny operator in the business of boyhood trading, my enthusiasm must have betrayed me. It was hard for me to conclude a deal, especially as I had little to offer, at least in trading-lines I might have the prospect of keeping secret from my parents.

Eventually, we did hit on an agreement. I even managed to persuade Ronnie to include his White's catalogue in his side of the bargain. My part of the agreement was more problematic. I had to put the electrodes from the controller of his train set onto the tip of my tongue. This worked from a twelve volt battery, so probably wouldn't have done any great harm. Still, I envisaged a painful snack. What I did was pretend to put the metal in my mouth although, in reality, I shielded it from my tongue with my thumbs. At the moment I did so, I twitched my head violently, in imitation of getting an electric shock.

This was it. Honour was satisfied, or at least it was satisfied as much as it was ever going to be. I was the new owner of the stamp.

I showed it to Jack, transferring my insane envy to him at a stroke. Together, we christened it 'The Sickie Vickie' and it became the undisputed jewel of both of our stamp collections. Over the next few months, he attempted to bargain for this prize. I delighted in his failed attempts. It gave me a sense of power.

Eventually, I relented. This wasn't through any generosity of spirit on my part. It was because he suggested an irresistible trade. He offered to give me a piggy-back ride for the entire length of our large local park. In those days I was small and light. Jack was far bigger. Nevertheless, it was some feat of strength and endurance for a ten-year-old. He deserved his reward, in the way the more churlish might say I never did.

I tried to avoid mentioning 'The Sickie Vickie' after that day. In reality, its monetary value was small. A good specimen is only now worth £10-£20 and this was far from being a good specimen (it is pictured on the cover). The franking may have been light, but the over-enthusiastic uncle, or some unknown earlier person, had cropped the stamp severely when removing it from the paper packaging all those years before.

My friend moved away from London a few years after this and I gave up stamp collecting soon afterwards. I tell myself this was because the Post Office had fallen prey to the business of issuing 'collector's sets'. In reality, it may have been more to do with the fact that I was missing the competitive element of philately.

*

Only a few years ago Jack, who had preserved his childhood album, unearthed it and brought it from his home in Sussex to show me. There was 'The Sickie Vickie', still on the page to which he had attached his trophy all those years before.

My daughter-in-law, who had lived in China until shortly before, happened to be in my home at the time. We showed her the album and tried to explain the significance of this grubby piece of paper. She didn't see what all the fuss was about.

Who would?

[26] The Yellow Omnibus

To combine poetry and handwriting lessons probably seemed like a good idea to some educationalists of the time. Quite economic and efficient in a way: the sort of thing that would appeal to a certain type of thinking today.

I was one of a class of forty or so nine-year-olds sitting, well-behaved, in a suburban schoolroom of the mid nineteen-fifties. It was a fine summer day, but we were ready to endure the last lesson before the fifteen or so minutes the teachers called break and we called playtime.

Mrs. Trevithick was really quite a good sort, usually able to inject a bit of life and meaning into dull lessons. She was short and plump, with quick movements and a manner which contrived to be friendly and aggressive at the same time. Her features were on the mannish side, but what you noticed about her was the mane of straw-coloured hair and her pale, watchful grey eyes. These would flicker in your direction when you thought it safe to doodle, to swap notes daringly scrawled with childish obscenities, or to pinch the girl sitting in front.

At this moment I was doing none of these things. Mrs. Trevithick was reading a poem with the title *Symphony in Yellow**. It was a short, simple piece, doing nothing cleverer than describing a scene in which this colour was the keynote. But for me, on that afternoon, this ordinary poem had a quality which can only be called magical.

Perhaps it was the enthusiasm my teacher brought to it; perhaps the afternoon sunlight streaming through the high windows made the moment itself a special one; perhaps it was merely the colour of the omnibus described in the poem – we would never have called our red monsters *omnibuses* – but the effect of that simple verse has stayed with me in a remarkable way. Even now I can, simply by closing my eyes, see that yellow omnibus coming through the fog and over the bridge. A great deal of far better writing has given me much reward since but none of it has had, nor I suppose ever will have, the same evocative quality.

Mrs. Trevithick read the poem three times, each time taking care and pleasure in it. As far as I was concerned she could have read it three times more. Instead, she closed the book suddenly and marched over to the blackboard in her brisk way.

The second part of the lesson had begun.

She continued to talk about the poem as she wrote it out on the board, swiftly and neatly, and seemingly from memory. But now she was talking more to distract her charges from their impulses toward waywardness than to impart a feeling for the poem, in the way she had a few minutes before.

Usually I resented copy work. I was often scolded for untidiness. This time I took more care than normal. I felt a definite thrill in writing out the word *omnibus*. My usual aim was to be one of the first to complete a handwriting task: Mrs. Trevithick often let the early finishers out into the yard a precious minute or two earlier. She was doing so on this day. Indeed, she was well on with her tour of inspection before I was half way through. But, keen as I was to join the other Cavaliers and Roundheads in their violent game, for once I did not hurry to finish.

When at last I was able to sit back with arms folded in the required fashion, I had produced what was by my standards a remarkably neat piece of copy. So I was surprised when Mrs. Trevithick surveyed my work with a critical eye; I was astounded when she pointed to the blackboard, then to my exercise book, and simply said:

'Do it again. Properly.'

This wasn't the first time I'd had to rewrite something. Once I'd recovered from my shock I set to work. All I could find wrong was one misspelling and a few capital letters carelessly used. This seemed small reason to have to repeat the exercise. It didn't take me long to do it, but the second time the task was joyless. *Omnibus* now was a series of marks I had to put down on the page because I'd been told to do it.

I couldn't believe it when my teacher's response to my second effort was an exasperated:

'No. Look at the board. Look!'

I really could not see what I was doing wrong. It was all I could do to choke back the tears of anger and frustration as I picked up my pen to begin once more the hated task. Only the child's fear of adult retribution drove me on.

After I had completed the first few lines, Mrs. Trevithick came to me and took the pen from my hand. More gently this time, she bade me look at the board. Still I could not see what was wrong. She walked slowly and silently to the board, and with her plump forefinger pointed very deliberately to the first word of each line in turn. Her hand followed a zigzag path and at last I could see my error.

Rhyming lines were carefully indented. So that, I naturally thought, was what made poetry different from other writing. Not the interplay and cadences of the words, not the power of imagery, not the unique pleasure to be had from the use of words like *omnibus*. Just a pretty pattern on the page.

Mrs. Trevithick did not have the heart to make me copy the thing again. She seemed to realise she had gone too far to make her point. She smiled as she finally relieved me of the exercise book and murmured a few words meant to be encouraging.

By then the whistle had blown in the yard, bringing to an end what was to be the last game of Cavaliers and Roundheads. One of the Roundheads had suffered a broken arm and the Headmaster, recognising the historical connections of the game were purely incidental, had banned it.

The Roundhead sported the distinction of a plaster cast for several weeks. A new game, Romans and Britons, had been initiated, enjoyed a short but vigorous life, and in its turn had been outlawed before the arm had healed. The damage to my literary sensibility was longer lasting. Although I developed a love of good writing, my preferences for many years were for prose. When I was well into my twenties my eyes would automatically skip over verse appearing in any text I was reading.

Eventually, I learned to resist this impulse, but even now I'm especially sensitive to the look of a piece on the page. A poem with many two- or three-word lines has to have some special aural or expressive qualities before it can start to have any chance with me. And all because of a prejudice I acquired over sixty years ago, in a sunlit schoolroom, and under the watchful eye of a teacher who, after all, was only doing her best.

> * *Symphony in Yellow* is a poem by Oscar Wilde, but I didn't know this at the time. I didn't even know who Oscar Wilde was then. As I've said, I think now it's a very ordinary poem. I don't mind rhyme at all, but Printer's Rhyme – rhyme looking as though it rhymes on the page (like 'wharf' and 'scarf' in Wilde's poem) but which doesn't when you say it – seems pointless to me. Anyway, here it is:

SYMPHONY IN YELLOW

Oscar Wilde

An omnibus across the bridge
    Crawls like a yellow butterfly,
    And, here and there, a passer-by
Shows like a little restless midge.

Big barges full of yellow hay
    Are moored against the shadowy wharf,
    And, like a yellow silken scarf,
The thick fog hangs along the quay.

The yellow leaves begin to fade
      And flutter from the Temple elms,
      And at my feet the pale green Thames
Lies like a rod of rippled jade.

[27] Dreamscapes

All my life I've had exotic dreams but those I experienced as a child were spectacularly weird. Some people tell me they dream in black and white. I never have. Indeed, I have sometimes dreamed in colours not found in the real spectrum. Don't ask me to describe them!

In the childhood dream remaining most vividly in my mind I was, for a reason I can't now remember, standing before a church window and carefully examining its stained glass. Suddenly, I found myself in two places at once. I was still looking at the glass in the normal way but I was also inside the picture it made.

The colours I saw and which surrounded the 'window-version' of me quickly became more intense than would ever be seen in a church or any other familiar place. The setting was one of a fragrant jungle (yes, I could smell it) with strange trees and other vegetation. All was set against a vividly deep blue sky.

To the 'observing' version of me, this scene was simply portrayed with sizeable pieces of coloured glass. No features were recognisable on my face in the window, even though my ground-based incarnation had no doubt it was me in the picture.

Gradually, everything seemed to animate and a lion bounded into the frame. I say 'bounded' but all was in extreme slow motion. Both versions of me became alarmed. The one in the window turned and tried to run. The problem was, he (or should I say I?) could only move very slowly, as if through an especially viscous liquid. I can't remember what happened after this. Presumably, in conventional dream fashion, I woke up.

In another dream, the colours were like those in a cartoon, though richer. But the landscape and figures weren't cartoon-like. They were utterly realistic. Although I wasn't aware of this when the dream began (if indeed there was such a point; dreams tend to blend into each other), I knew as the dream progressed I had to keep climbing a spiralling wooden staircase. The staircase was inside the centre of a stone tower and it took a very long time for me to ascend. Eventually, I did reach a doorway. This I opened and was both surprised and yet not surprised to see, an astronomer with his telescope pointed through the single large window. I knew the man was an astronomer, although he was dressed in the cloak of the wizard of fairy tales. He smiled warmly and beckoned me over to the window.

As I approached the window of the astronomer's room I was entranced to see a huge, bright orange disc hanging in the sky. Although it was featureless, and far brighter even than the unrealistic picture on my bagatelle game at home, I knew I was seeing the Planet Mars.

Without hesitation, I looked through the telescope. In waking life, I wasn't to look through anything that could remotely qualify as an astronomical telescope for another few years, and then it was only at our Moon. At this point, I lost all sense of size and proportion. I could see part of the disc, still entirely featureless.

Bouncing freely about on the surface were semi-transparent cartoon-like beings, not unlike kangaroos with giant ears but no legs. They were as if drawn in thick black outlines with a kind of yellow halo effect. I remember feeling pleased at being the discoverer of life on other worlds before the dream faded out or more likely was transformed into something quite different. I know I didn't wake up immediately on this occasion.

This dream was so realistic that when I did wake I was convinced I really had found life on another planet. I tried to work out the best way to break this sensational news to the World. Should I tell my family first? Would they believe me? Not too quickly, I came to realise that it all must have been a dream after all. Reluctantly, I came to accept that the Martian beings would have to be some hundreds of miles high for me to be able to view them in the way I did.

At all events, I was delighted by what I had seen. For a few years past, I had been fascinated by every aspect of the night sky. As well as staring above me when outside, whenever the cloud cover allowed – even in outer London there was far less interference from artificial light than there is now in small towns like the one where I live now. I would also read every book or anything else I could get hold of connected with the heavens, scientific or otherwise.

My 'studies' were formless and ill-directed, although I did learn some concrete facts along with much dross. I did, for instance, discover how to recognise a number of the constellations and knew in which seasons they appeared. The knowledge I have now is essentially a more sophisticated but watered-down version of that I acquired in my first decade.

One of my favourite toys at that time was a cheap plastic bagatelle game. The object of this was to fire white marbles into cups, above which were representations of planetary discs. Apart from the ring around Saturn (there are in fact several), these bore little relation to the images of the planets we can actually see through a telescope.

Although I was familiar with more realistic portrayals and even blurred photographs in books, I was half-convinced that Jupiter was a bright blue and Neptune a dirty grey. The score was higher for landing marbles in the more difficult targets. Pluto, as one of the smaller as well as the most distant planet, was worth 10,000 points. I was disappointed when, in my adult years, Pluto was declassified from major planetary status and had its estimated diameter halved. Mars was depicted as an altogether unrealistic orange globe. I can't remember how many points this was worth but I'm sure this illustration was the genesis of my dream.

Among the odd but definitely pleasurable dreams were some dark ones. I have written about the scariest in *Frightening the Children* (see [14] so won't repeat myself here. That one seemed to last a very long time, though fortunately all the others I recall would have to be described as brief, if intense.

The strange entities I encountered in these dreams were mainly enhanced versions of those I saw on the pages of comics, or in an old, very large book of ghost stories that belonged to my family and was kept hidden from me. At least the family thought it was hidden from me; I found it and spent long, secret times, scaring myself by marvelling at the black-and-white line drawings on some of its large, creased pages.

My particular favourite was a drawing of a ghostly horse thrusting its head through an open window, terrifying the people in the house. This image migrated from the book to my dreams more than a few times.

If you are nodding sagely at this point, let me tell you that my darker dreams also featured a Welsh bible, bought on the occasion of the wedding of my maternal grandparents at the beginning of the twentieth century and until this millennium still in my family, plus a strange book called the *Ludwigs of Bavaria*, come from goodness knows where. In the latter case I was fascinated by the name 'Ludwig' and the musty smell of the book. Neither volume contained illustrations, although the Bible did include one highly coloured page featuring the Lord's Prayer in a dozen other languages, one of which was English.

I know I am far from unique in having dreams in which I have the power of flight. In fact I still have them, though these days my elevated manoeuvres are usually restricted to gliding or long-hopping at most six feet off the ground. When I regularly had 'proper' flying dreams I didn't zoom about, Superman fashion. Instead I floated quite sedately above the ground at heights which must have varied from fifty to thousands of feet.

My interest always lay more in what was on the ground beneath me than the mere fact I could fly. I accepted this as entirely normal and was slightly surprised when I couldn't do it in the day. The scenes below me were either strange and unworldly or quite mundane. For instance, one fairly frequent dream I experienced featured me flying over a smoky, blue-grey planet and wondering whether I should descend beneath the clouds to see what lay below. I never did. Another had me flying at a height of no more than fifty feet over the shopping crowds in West Ealing and Ealing Broadway, a few miles from where I lived.

I'm not sure at what stage in my life I found my night-time aerial antics severely restricted. Probably it was a gradual process. There must be some sort of parallel with the actual process of ageing and getting more responsible there!

[28] Ban the Bomb

If I'd been familiar with the expression back in April, 1958, I'd have said what I could see before me in Trafalgar Square was a sea of faces. And not only faces: there were banners, a white haired man addressing the vast crowd through an erratic microphone and numerous eye catching black-and-white CND 'bird's foot' symbols.

This scene was something I'd come across entirely by chance. In my wanderings around London, the name 'Trafalgar Square' on the tube station sign must have triggered some youthful resonance – more likely with the 'Monopoly' board than any historical connection or thoughts of Nelson's column – and I'd emerged from the underground to explore the area.

The idea of a ten-year-old roaming unaccompanied around London today would have people sending for the social workers in a panic. Back then it wasn't so unusual. For the year or so previously, there'd been few things I'd liked better than to explore far and wide; this included the countryside as well as the city. Most often I would do it in the company of a friend or two but, if they all preferred to spend their precious pocket money on such frivolities as a visit to the sweetshop, I was quite happy to venture out alone.

As soon as I saw it, I wanted to be part of the event. For this I cannot claim any kind of early political awareness. I was able to glean no more than the vaguest idea of what it was all about; I certainly didn't recognise the white haired man as Bertrand Russell. If someone had told me who he was, my likely response would have been, 'who's he then?'

So, I pressed forward into the heart of the crowd. This was easy enough to do: there were plenty of children who were part of the throng. There were even babies and infants in prams and pushchairs. The fact that most of the others were accompanied was of no great moment. There were numerous police officers around, but they were good humoured and went about their duties with a light touch.

The whole thing was immensely attractive to me. The duffel coats, the black jumpers and the slogans all weaved their magic spell. Most appealing were the young girls who, in my distorted adult memory, all had long dark hair. A few days after this I read in an outraged newspaper report to the effect that 'often the young men and women shared a sleeping bag'. I didn't then appreciate the significance of this but all the same the act struck me as defiant and romantic. And I do mean 'romantic' rather than 'sexual'.

I fell in with a group of teenagers. There were two girls and a bearded young man in heavily framed glasses who had an intense expression but said very little. Both of the girls had long, dark hair. Perhaps this is why in my memory all of the girls gathered in Trafalgar Square on that day live on as carefree, arty brunettes.

They told me they were marching to Aldermaston to protest against nuclear weapons. This was the first CND Easter March. It was routed from London to Aldermaston rather than the other way around, as it was to be in future years. Immediately I said I'd be marching, too. In reply to questions about whether my mother would be worried, I waved my hand vaguely in the direction of the other side of the square and said, 'Oh, my mother and father are coming along. They're over there.' They weren't of course: they were safely at home. In three or four hours they might start to get concerned about my absence, though not before.

After what seemed to be an age of speeches, the crowd started to move off. Because of the numbers involved, progress was slow. I confess I was already seriously bored by the time we'd left the environs of Trafalgar Square.

'How far is Aldermaston, then?' I asked.

'It's in Berkshire. About thirty or forty miles, I should think'. These were almost the first words the bearded man had spoken.

Thirty or forty miles? This seemed like the other side of the world to me. I had visions of another parental inquisition if I were late home for dinner. When we had marched for far less than a mile, I saw another tube station and slipped away, guiltily.

*

The CND protests were a phenomenon of their time. They probably made little if any difference to practical politics, even if they represented the voice of social conscience in what was – and we shouldn't forget this – the age of the balance of terror.

My only other act for CND was to deliver a few leaflets many years later, as an adult living in Wales. I confess that even this action was driven more by nostalgia than political belief. There are idle moments today when I catch myself dreaming of a thing that has nothing to do with the aims of CND. Did the group of teenagers I met in 1958 have two sleeping bags or an enormous one suitable for three people? And, if the former, could a romantically misguided ten-year-old have managed somehow to squeeze himself into one of them with a long haired brunette?

[29] Fragments

Unlike the other pieces here, this doesn't even pretend to be on a particular theme or topic or to present a consistent narrative. It is made up from my recollections of a number of disparate memories from the nineteen-fifties.

<u>SEEING A GHOST?</u>

I have a number of memories of apparently supernatural experience from the decade. For most of them, a reasonable, rational explanation could be put forward. Not this one, I think.

At the age of around seven or eight, or at any rate when I was trusted to bath myself but not to run the bathwater at the correct temperature, my mother was filling the bath and called me upstairs. The bathroom light was on so I didn't bother to switch on that of the staircase. As I reached three-quarters of the way to the top, an odd two-dimensional shape 'swam' through the outside wall on my right, in front of my face, and through the bedroom wall to my left.

<u>WARLIKE BEHAVOUR</u>

It was the practice during my first year at infants' school to allow pupils to bring in toys from home on a Friday. One boy, called Derek, brought in a highly impressive fort and soldiers set. Through envy I suppose, I went over to him twice and knocked his soldiers over. Soon after this, he left the school and moved away to Reading. Later, he returned to my town. He joined a different primary school, but funnily enough we were in the same class in Senior School. And we were friends!

FOUR-AND-TWENTY

The first jig-saw puzzle I owned and completed, not very long before I started school, had 24 pieces. It was based on the nursery rhyme beginning, 'four and twenty blackbirds baked in a pie' and had this motto at the bottom. This was probably the only jig-saw I've completed unaided in my life. I'm not a fan!

THE BLUE PERIOD

In the first 'art lesson' I recall from my infants' school, I decided to paint a picture of a red sports car I'd seen on the way to school that morning. It was going to be a great picture; the fact that I had only blue powder paint was purely incidental. What put me off was the way my diluted paint ran down the paper on the easel.

1066 AND ALL THAT

So inspired was I by a history lesson that I drew a scene from the Battle of Hastings. This pictured the moment when Harold was killed by an arrow in the eye, naturally. I went on adding arrows to the picture until there was a veritable hail of them. Then, over the next few weeks, I went on adding arrows until they'd almost obscured the drawing.

PICKLED SWIMMING

When I was about ten, a group of three or four friends and I started to go swimming. We went in the fourpenny baths because it was the cheapest (the grander ones cost sixpence and ninepence). At that time, unlike most of the others, I couldn't swim and splashed about in the shallow end. No matter: I enjoyed the bus ride home and the chips and pickles we always bought far more.

LIFE AND LIMB

During the Easter Holiday of 1952, shortly after he'd started school (I wasn't to begin until the following November) Paul, the friend my mother looked after persuaded me to 'come and have a look at the canal'. We were found by the adults with our heads and shoulders poking through the railings of the bridge.

During his school summer holiday that year, I persuaded *him* to make a return visit. I monkeyed across the pipe spanning the canal. He didn't; he was 'chubby'. It seemed a very risky feat to me only a few years later. A couple of years ago I came across a photograph of the old bridge, replaced c1960. This confirms my opinion.

THE KING IS DEAD

I was born during the reign of King George VI but have no memories of his reign. In fact my first memory of him came shortly after his death, in 1952. There was a letter on our sideboard, with a stamp bearing his portrait. My mother said, 'they'll have to change the stamps now the King's dead'.

EVOLUTION

My favourite lesson in my junior school, partly because its centrepiece was a radio programme, was *How Things Began*. In this we were taught firmly that the first Hominid on Earth was 'Peking Man'. In later years, it took me some time to accept things could be otherwise and that the cradle of mankind might really be Africa. At least we weren't taught that the Earth was made in 4004 BC.

FA CUP DAY, 1956

In the days when we hadn't altogether eschewed the 'pretty pictures' variety of philately, my friend Jack and I walked the mile to our local town to buy what used to be known as a 'short set' of the Monaco commemorative issues issued a few weeks before to mark the wedding of Prince Rainier and Princess Grace. It was called a 'short set' because we could only afford the two cheapest of the four stamps, the green and the red. Although it was only May, it was a very hot day and I all but keeled over when I reached home to watch the FA cup final on TV with a much-needed glass of water in my hand.

BUS STRIKE

Working for London Transport in 1958, my father was one of those involved in the strike. All this meant for our family was financial hardship; the industrial action lasted for several weeks. Towards its end, the son of one of my mother's friends from the Rhondda Fach came to stay with us for a long weekend. On the Saturday he, Geraint, came with us to visit my Aunt and Uncle who lived about five miles away. This time, the journey involved a long walk to a local railway station to catch the 'Pull 'n' Pull Push' steam train. After Geraint had returned home, there was much grumbling from my parents because he'd allowed my father to 'put his hand in his pocket and pay for his ticket' (this was the expression they used) at a time of difficulty. I'd been about to suggest that we always made the journey by train instead of by boring bus. When I heard this I thought better of it. I knew my father had free travel on the buses.

PRE-WAR

When I was very young, my mother called in to see a friend of hers. The women wanted to talk, so I was deposited in the other room, in front of the gas fire. This was off, so it couldn't have been in the winter. The house was dark and gloomy even so, and I was uncomfortable in it. To keep me quiet, I was given a small metal fire engine to play with. It was impressed on me that it had belonged to the son of my mother's friend and had been made BEFORE THE WAR (I heard this phrase in capitals). It was crudely made and surely couldn't have born much relation to an actual road vehicle. When we left, I was presented with this toy amid much fuss. I never played with it again.

PRE-TV

One evening when I was very young, not long after I'd gone to bed, there was a thunderstorm that frightened me. I went downstairs and was received sympathetically: my mother said something about me being 'nearer to the storm up there'. The household was busy in what we grandly called 'the dining-room'. Actually, it was the family's main living-room; at that time we followed the Welsh practice of keeping the front room 'for best'. In practice, this meant 'for never'.

I can't remember what my father and sister were doing, but my mother was writing one of her letters (she was an inveterate letter-writer to family and friends in Wales and further afield) and my brother was building a sleek model aeroplane from brown paper. I marvelled at what was going on; it seemed much more interesting than the life I was used to in the daytime. Next night I tried to come down again. There was no thunderstorm and they wouldn't let me.

THE RACECOURSE

During my first year in school, a classmate of mine, Basil Jones, whom I picture (probably unfairly) as forever crying, was going to move away. His mother, who worked in the local newsagent, explained to me they were moving away to live 'on the racecourse'. This sounded exciting to me, though I did wonder what the horses would make of all that crying. Not until a few years later did I understand that 'The Racecourse' was the name of a new housing estate. It was built on the site of a pony track which had operated in the nineteen-thirties.

DOUBLE YOUR BROTHERS

Until the elder came home from the army on leave, I was only in theory aware I had two big brothers. The elder regaled me with stories of firing shots over the heads of camels in Egypt and brought me a harmonica from Hamburg. He also made me be the witness when he ceremonially burnt a photograph of a German girl with whom he'd parted company.

WHO WANTS TO BE A MILLIONAIRE?

One day, my parents took me to visit my mother's maternal aunt and cousin who lived a few miles away. The cousin, a year or so younger than my mother, presented me with, literally, millions of Marks from the Weimar Republic's inflationary days. He was passing on to me what he called a 'sovaneer' from his time as a soldier in post-war Germany. I was impressed with all this money, but it didn't stop me from trading the notes away over the next few weeks. I probably realised more value than the banknotes' monetary worth in my wheeler-dealing.

MAGIC

The younger of my two brothers liked to send me far and wide on exotic procurement missions. I loved it. One I remember in particular was to buy the pre-army but otherwise undistinguished Elvis record *Let's Have a Party*. This was only a purchase from a local record shop but I travelled much further by 'tube' train for him. A journey I made several times before and after the record purchase was to a joke and novelty shop in Holborn, London for him. This was called Ellisdson's and had, I remember, two or three floors. What I liked about these longer trips, as well as the adventure of the journey, was that I was allowed a shilling or more to buy something for myself. I was attracted to the 'magic tricks' although they never seemed to work properly.

IT'S MORE THAN ROCK 'N' ROLL

I was no more than vaguely aware of the dawning of Rock. I might not have noticed but for a change in the record collections of my siblings. I would give the discs an unauthorised playing when I could. As well as Bill Haley records like *Rock Around the Clock*, *See You Later Alligator*, *Green Tree Boogie* and early Elvis records like *Hound Dog*, I especially liked Caterina Valente's *The Breeze and I*, Frankie Laine's *Jealousy* and Ernie Ford's *Sixteen Tons*.

In the nineteen-eighties my two young sons picked up the lyrics of the last named from me and sang lines like 'I was born one morning when the sun didn't shine' everywhere to their mother's consternation. My absolute favourites were several Fats Domino records and *St Louis Blues*. This I thought was sung by someone called WC Handy. His name must have been on the record label as the composer.

[30] The Call of the Sea: *[II] The Pier's End*

Our time in Porthcawl in 1952, wet as it was, had given me an appetite for seaside holidays. I thought they were to be an annual event and was disappointed when I found otherwise. It was to be another two years before I saw the sea again, and then it was only for a day.

A year or so before we went to Porthcawl, my father changed his employment. His previous job was with the local Gas Board. He'd worked for its predecessor pre-war and after army service. His new job was working on the buses of London Transport. This wasn't better or more highly paid employment. In fact, in some ways it was worse. It involved shift work. My father made the move because he was becoming increasingly nervous about working as a gas fitter when he had no sense of smell. Ironically, some years later the nation switched from poisonous town gas to the non-toxic, odourless North Sea gas. Although perhaps it wasn't so ironic because soon after the Gas Boards, in our case the North Thames Gas Board, inserted a smell, albeit a less offensive one.

My father's change of job made little difference to my own life. He was either on 'earlies' or 'lates' and was often required to work on a Sunday. In fact, I rather liked it when his 'rest day' was on a Friday. Then he would be required to go to a nearby bus garage to pick up his wages. Until I started school, I travelled free and could go with him. It wasn't a great distance but involved a change of buses. I saw it as a great adventure, the highlight of which was a cup of tea in the canteen. The tea was stewed, disgusting stuff, but this didn't deter me. I never did like tea but forced myself to swallow the whole mugful. It was part of the adventure.

Best of all for me about my father's new job was that, after he had been working for London Transport for a few years, Sunday excursions were organised for staff and their families. The red double-decker buses would assume a 'Private Hire' message to replace their normal destination signs. They'd be driven to exotic places instead of along their usual mundane routes. Eastbourne, Southsea and Ramsgate are a few that have burnt particular images in my mind, favourable, unfavourable and downright strange.

In 1955, my parents again decided to go for a caravan holiday, this time to Clacton-on-sea. On this occasion, an Aunt and Uncle of mine were to accompany us. They were to be my parents' holiday companions for the next fifteen or so years, long after I preferred to go independently. I've mentioned the Clacton holiday in the introductory piece, so won't do so at length here.

I would like to observe, though, that I've seen photographs of the caravan we hired, and am amazed to think how five people fitted into it, comfortably as far as I remember. It was small: only about three times the size of the tin can we hired in Porthcawl. The other thing that baffles me from an adult perspective is how seriously the five of us (I was allowed a voice) discussed the relative merits of the nearby and quite similar resorts we visited on day trips. These were, I remember, St Osyth, Jaywick and Walton-on-the-Naze. The last was deemed to be 'the best', although even at the time I couldn't have said why.

It was another three years before we went away again for a seaside holiday. In 1958, the destination was Maidencombe, a short distance to the north of Torquay. Again the five of us stayed in a caravan. This time it was bigger and considerably more comfortable, though it was still lit by Calor gas. This was the normal thing in those days and my constant memory of those times is the low hiss of gas burning in the fragile and low-light mantle. To me, it seems odd indeed that 'gaslighting' now has an altogether different and more sinister definition, that of psychological abuse. This developed from the nineteen-thirties play, *Gaslight* and its later film adaption starring Ingrid Bergman, Charles Boyer and Joseph Cotten.

A steep path led down to a small beach of reddish shingle. The bathing area was wonderfully sheltered and I was content to walk down to it as often as I could. In contrast to our holiday in Porthcawl, the weather was sunny and hot for most of our fortnight. This isn't a 'sun was always shining' memory. I was inclined to spend too much time on the little beach. One day, back in the caravan, I collapsed with heatstroke after spending hours in the sun.

The other strong memory I have of the fortnight concerns the book my uncle was reading in the caravan. It was a paperback version of Bram Stoker's *Dracula*. I was fascinated by the gleaming eyes of the Count on the cover and would 'borrow' the book so I could read furtive chunks as often as I could. It wasn't until towards the end of the fortnight, when I'd read about three-quarters of it, that my surreptitious reading was discovered and prohibited. Not for some weeks after I'd returned home was I able to secure another copy and complete my reading of the novel. I've read it a few times in adult years. Whether it should be called a great book may be debateable, although it does remain the creepiest I've read.

I'd have been happy to spend every day on Maidencombe Beach, but often the adults dragged me out on day trips. The three big resorts of Torbay, together with Babbacombe, Oddicombe and Teignmouth are the ones I remember. We also went on a cruise along the River Dart, and I still recall the adults pointing out 'Greenway', Agatha Christie's holiday home in the valley of the River Dart. At the time, the detective writer was still using it. Since it was summer, she may even have been there. I had not a clue as to who she could be. I thought of 'Aunt Agatha', of 'Lord Snooty and his Pals', a weekly strip in the Beano comic.

The next year we took a ferry across the Solent to the Isle of Wight and had a week in Shanklin. Things were a little different this time; we didn't stay in a caravan but in a seaside guest house. Unlike the traditional landlady of the comic postcards, Mrs Cotton was patient and tolerant. I was under strict orders to behave myself and for once the plain British cooking didn't give me any trouble. Rather than have me performing at the dining room table, my parents gave me permission to unload the things I didn't like onto their plates.

We went to various resorts around the Island beside Shanklin. They all seemed the same to me; I'd have been happy to stay local. I did like the 'Pedalo' craft, summer gardens and 'Chine' rambles. Alum Bay seemed a magical place because of the coloured sands; I thought all sand was sand-coloured. The walk between Shanklin and neighbouring Sandown seemed like a major undertaking to me, although in reality it was no more than a stroll. We didn't visit Queen Victoria's Osborne House in East Cowes, a thing I'd like to have done for some reason but wasn't to achieve for another fifty years.

My strongest memory of the fortnight was toward the end of our holiday. One evening we went to the end of the pier to see a local character called 'Daredevil Lawrence'. The pier has gone now: it was finally demolished in 1993 after lingering in a wraith like form following the storms of 1987. But, in 1959, it was the centrepiece of the resort.

Daredevil Lawrence's speciality was to dive from the end of the pier. What made this enterprise special was that one of his arms had been amputated at the elbow, I believe as the result of a war wound. Following a massive build-up involving much speechifying and rattling of Lawrence's collecting tin, he duly dived into the sea. After this, he rather detracted from the build-up by encouraging all the teenagers present to jump into the sea. Many did. I dearly wanted to join them. At eleven years old, I was a sort of teenager, wasn't I? But I knew my parents would never allow it. Besides, at that age, I couldn't swim.

I do tend to think of 1959 as my last holiday with my parents. To be historically accurate, I should say it wasn't. The summer afterwards, I had my first 'independent' holiday when I went to North Devon with the Boy Scouts for two weeks. When I returned I lodged for a fortnight with a friend's family while my parents enjoyed their own holiday. But 1959 wasn't even the last time I went with them, because I accompanied the quartet of adults twice more. In 1961 I was deeply bored on a dull site in a duller coastal town in Hampshire called Milford-on-Sea.

As late as 1964 we stayed in a comparatively luxurious caravan in Poole. On that occasion, though, I took my friend Dave with me and we went our own way. In fact we both had examination commitments and travelled down to Dorset a couple of days after the four adults. Our bedroom was sealed off from the rest of the accommodation so in reality we didn't do much more than share most meals. Certainly I had no bucket and spade on the beach or model boat in the sea.

So, to me, it has always seemed my childhood started its end on Shanklin Pier in the summer of 1959.

[31] End of Innocence

In the summer of 1960, near Berrynarbor on the North Devon coast, I was with my companions from a Boy Scouts' Troop, spending a two-week 'Summer Camp' on a farm.

I don't know if all Boy Scout Troops were the same in 1960, or if mine were exceptionally purist, but we took the outdoor life very seriously. All of our cooking was done by we boys on an open fire; all our washing (both of clothes and bodies) was done in a stream; we transported our mass of semi-military equipment in a wooden handcart we had to push along a road to a railway station. This wasn't our local railway station, either.

The only concession to the mid-Twentieth Century I remember was that we were allowed to light our camp fire each morning with matches. Most of us had already gained our sew-on fire-lighting badges. The task we had to perform to earn these entailed the building and lighting of a fire without artificial aids.

Yet I loved all this back-to-nature stuff, as did the other boys. Baden-Powell would have been proud of us. Certainly we looked down upon the members of the Boys' Brigade, who were rumoured to be mollycoddled on their summer camps with bell-tents, full-size gas stoves and, unbelievably, adult cooks to use them.

On this afternoon, though, I was far from happy. The morning had seen our sole modern 'treat' of the fortnight. We'd been allowed a coach trip to the fair in Minehead, where we were free to enjoy guilty pleasures like the Dodgem Cars for a few hours. More importantly, we'd been permitted to wear jeans over the khaki shorts of our uniforms.

I cannot convey to you the significance of this. Realising they were losing scouts in droves by forcing boys in their early- to mid-teens to walk the streets in shorts, HQ (whoever they were) had decreed we could wear jeans over our shorts to attend the scout hall. We were doing our best to extend this to all public appearances.

That morning, I had been the sole member of our troop to wear shorts to the fair in Minehead. This was because, on the previous evening, I had slithered on the backside of my only pair of jeans into a wet pancake laid on a hillside by an inconsiderate cow. Immediately afterwards, presumably seeking consolation, I had stolen a spoonful of jam from the large tin used to store it and had swallowed a wasp in the process. At least, I was convinced it was a wasp and this was what mattered. I was quite sure I could feel twinges in my throat and gullet, without being precisely sure where my gullet was.

In the later afternoon, back from Minehead, I found myself alone in the camp while the others were on some sort of stonecraft (whatever that was) mission. After the noise of the fair, I admit I was enjoying the tranquillity.

It was my turn to return to camp early to boil a Billy-can of water for tea, so I'd left the other boys to explore the local beach without me. I felt this to be unfair: I had been the one who'd been allotted the Billy-can duties only two days before. True, on that occasion it was because I'd lost a singing-game but, as far as I was concerned, this should have excused me from taking my scheduled turn. To me, this was especially so since I was convinced I'd encountered a ghost on my previous solo duty. I hadn't yet told any of the others of this experience but I was fearful of being in the camp on my own again, even in broad daylight.

Such was the resentful swirl of my emotions as I stood on the threshold of our camp. My intention was to wash the besmeared jeans, something I hadn't been granted leave to do on the previous evening. The Scoutmaster probably wanted me to avoid any temptation to wear the damp jeans to Minehead. This I can reason as an adult, but at the age of twelve I put it down to sheer vindictiveness on his part.

I managed to put my resentments and fears to one side and strode forward to tackle my stained jeans. I despaired when I saw and smelled the brown blemishes. In the event, the stains proved easy to remove in the clear waters of the stream. At least, the waters were clear when I began the operation. They soon became discoloured, especially when I used some contraband washing-powder to hasten the stains away.

Then I saw it. Not more than twenty yards upstream was a silver shape in the water. It was a small trout. I thought immediately of catching it by tickling. I had no idea how I should go about such a task. This didn't matter in the slightest. I crept upstream, lay on my belly, and moved my fingers vaguely under the trout's body.

Emboldened by the fish's quietude, I gently closed my fingers around its slender six-inch form and hoisted it clear of the water. It gave barely a wriggle. I looked at it, and saw it was boldly marked in the fashion of one I'd seen illustrated in a book from my local library. It was sleekly glistening from the stream, now quite clear again after my depredations with the jeans.

What should I do? What I did was gently replace the trout in mid-stream and repeated my 'tickling' exercise. I did this six times more before I realised the trout must be very sick indeed to be so co-operative.

Then, from the corner of my eye, I could see I was being watched by somebody standing in the exact spot I'd occupied an hour before. It was Terry Lenaghan. I left my living plaything in the water, quickly got to my feet, and gave my jeans one further wringing onto the grass.

Terry Lenaghan was my bitterest enemy. He'd occupied that position since the previous week, when I'd demolished his older brother Mick in a fight. Terry's resentment was mainly silent. This didn't matter. He and I both knew he'd have to seek family vengeance as soon as the opportunity presented itself. Now that opportunity had arrived.

It didn't matter that Terry was several months younger than me and about eighteen months younger than Mick. I knew he'd be an altogether different prospect. He was a tough kid. The fact that he'd seen me thrash his elder brother in quick-time would only make him angry and more determined.

Sure enough, Terry strode over to where I was standing and raised his fists, without wasting time on the verbal insults we boys usually saw as a necessary preliminary to the fine art of roughhousing. In response I raised my own fists. I said nothing. What could I say?

He squared up to me with a high guard. I had the horrible thought that Mr Lenaghan; the boys' father might have been a more successful boxing coach with his younger son than he was a football coach to our Scout Troop. He looked more like an ex-boxer than an ex-footballer. Terry didn't. He looked like a boxer *now*.

We danced around each other, feinting ineffectually. Then Terry let fly a punch that landed, quite lightly, on my right side. Immediately I responded with a punch of my own, equally light. This was getting ridiculous. If I didn't get flattened, I might end up looking stupid. Then I had a brainwave.

'Would you like me to show you how to tickle a trout?' I said, holding my hands up in the air to show a truce.

'What?' said Terry, surprised.

'How to tickle a trout. That's what I'm talking about. I can show you how it's done. Not many people know how to do it.'

'*You* don't know how to catch a trout.' Terry still had his boxer's guard up.

'Bet you I do. There's a trout in the stream now.'

Terry's curiosity was piqued. He glanced over toward the stream and dropped his guard.

'Go on, then,' he said. 'You realise I'm letting you do this because you're the only other one in the camp?'

'I'm doing it because *you're* the only other one in the camp.'

Fortunately the trout was in the same part of the stream, obligingly still in mid-water. I beckoned Terry to follow, making great play of our stealthy approach. Then I lay down on my stomach, and gingerly hoisted the trout out of the water. Terry looked on, entranced. His hated enemy had taken on the status of a magician.

'Think you can do it?' I said, adopting a superior tone, as if I were a senior scout teaching a 'Tenderfoot' a new knot. 'You have to get your hand under its belly without the fish noticing'.

The trout was probably too dazed to know or care how it was being handled and allowed Terry to lift it out of the stream three times. It was surely nearing the end of its young life.

'That's enough. You don't want to affect the breeding. It's a hen you know.' The fish was probably both too young and too infirm to breed. I didn't know whether it was breeding season or not. Nor did I have a clue as to its sex. By pure chance I happened to know the correct term for a female fish. My knowledgeable pronouncement certainly impressed Terry.

After that, we became firm friends. Terry helped me with the final wringing-out of my jeans and put the water on the fire to boil. We pottered around the camp like the mates we were. Terry gave me the dried-out shell of a crab's claw he had picked up from the local beach. Our camaraderie lasted for at least thirty minutes.

*

'Let's go and tickle that trout again,' said Terry.

I had no enthusiasm for this. The fish might have been dead by now, I reasoned. But I allowed Terry to lead the way back to the stream, not wishing to be labelled a spoil-sport. When we reached the stream, there was no sign of the young fish. But we found something else.

'What's that?' we said together.

We could both see well enough what it was. In the water, at the point where the stream left a small copse, was a forearm clad in a half rolled up pink sleeve. We saw the blanched and wrinkled hand of a young girl.

After no more than a minute or two the rest of our Troop, our Scoutmaster Ted at its head, noisily arrived back in the camp.

Immediately, I ran over to him and blurted out the story of our grisly discovery. My explanation was incoherent but he understood the key facts readily enough. He detailed two of the senior boys to run for the local police.

'Terry Lenaghan was with me,' I said. I glanced back over my shoulder. There was no sign of Terry Lenaghan.

'You'd better go and take it easy in the tent,' said Ted.

*

Inside the tent, I had one thought. Terry must have done it. This was my bizarre conclusion. Why else would he have made himself scarce when the others appeared? But how could I betray my friend?

Most of the Scouts in our Troop were Catholics. It was strictly non-denominational; in fact this was the reason why there were so many Catholics among our number. Unlike all the other Scout Troops in our area, ours wasn't attached to a Church. I had heard that you could make a confession to a Catholic Priest and rely on him not to repeat the story to the Police. Perhaps I could ask one of the Catholic boys how to go about making a confession. But to what exactly would I confess?

*

Within the hour, someone I assumed to be a detective came into the tent. I couldn't help noticing he had a small boil on his upper lip and had made a clumsy job of shaving around it.

'So, you're the one who found the body, are you?'

'Yes,' I said, without hesitation. Terry and I had found it together, but I didn't say anything to him about this.

He asked me a few other questions: name and address; when I had come to Berrynarbor; what I'd been doing earlier in the day. None of the questions seemed incisive to me. Not once during the ten minutes the detective remained in the tent did I mention Terry's name.

I was pleased about my steadfastness and group loyalty. But, after I was left alone again, I began to worry. What if, in my efforts to protect Terry, I had caused suspicion to fall on me? Would 'the code' mean I'd have to take the blame silently? After all, this wasn't a scrumping raid or truancy we were talking about. Terry hadn't said a word to me before his disappearing act.

*

I went through agonies of self-examination and doubt before the Scoutmaster reappeared with explanations.

The young girl had not been murdered by anyone. She'd disappeared from her home a week or so before we set up camp. She was it seemed one of those unfortunates they dismissively labelled at the time 'slow'. A large-scale police search had failed to find her. Now they were satisfied that she'd fallen accidentally somewhere upstream and her body had been washed down to where we'd found it. They were quite sure it was an accident and she'd died before any of us had set foot in North Devon.

The next day the girl's mother arrived at the camp to offer her tearful thanks. It was a distressing scene, all the more so when the Scoutmaster singled me out as 'the boy who found your poor daughter'. Terry was impassive during this visit.

*

Now, though, I had to re-join the other boys. The police were still there, fussing around some screening cloth they'd clumsily erected around the place where we'd found the corpse. Terry was chattering to his friends and watching the police activity from a distance. I caught his eye. He smirked, turned his back on me, and carried on with his conversation.

Appendix I

Memory

What is memory?
Someone mentions Norfolk;
Norfolk is in East Anglia.
And in my hand is a paper packet,
East Anglia Crisps proclaimed on the side.
I am nine years old and
all I see is that packet
and that the place, Clacton it was,
had two big dippers.
A thing of no consequence even then.
Yet take me there,
show me there is only one,
and a small building-block flakes away.
Take away too many and
the edifice itself will crumble.

Appendix II

The Father of my Uncle

Yes, I recall my uncle's father, the old man in the chair.
He had white dusty hair
and died when I was three,
as if he'd never been there.

He'd sit all day in the dark parlour
regarding the world with disfavour
and not a single trace of humour.

He wore a brown tobacco-smelling suit,
though I never saw him with a light
and I never saw him smoke.
He never shared a joke;
I never heard him speak.
Could be he'd lost the touch;
perhaps in all those years he'd seen too much.

We had no ties of blood:
his grandsire had crossed the sea from far Tralee,
a place where no roses grow;
and where even the life-giving potato
had rotted in the mud.

The old man had left a London slum
for the Rhondda, with his gin-soaked wife
and my uncle, in those days his toddler son,
because he'd heard the streets were paved with coal
but all he'd found was grief and strife
and there he grew old.

One day, he rose from his seat near the mantel
to stumble down the passageway.
Amazed to find he could move at all,
I followed him, until he fell back upon me.

My mother screamed: 'He's killed him!'
I thought: 'I've killed him.'
But my mother was thinking of me;
she thought the old man had put out my light.

But maybe I was right:
the father of my uncle died when I was three.

Recently by Tom East

NOVELS
The Gospel According to St Judas
The Greenland Party
Tommy's War: July, 1914

THE ELDRITCH COLLECTIONS
The Eve of St Eligius
Wish Man's Wood

OTHER FICTION
Dimension Five

POETRY
Scenes from Seasons
Charge of The Light Verse Brigade
Lyrics, Polemics & Poetics

*Coming later in 2020,
a dark novel:
The Ka of Stephen Charles*

CPSIA information can be obtained
at www.ICGtesting.com
Printed in the USA
LVHW081043130320
649970LV00004B/340